MAKING GAMES FOR THE NES®

An 8bitworkshop Book

Steven Hugg, Author   Jennifer Harvey, Editor

July 2022

MAKING GAMES FOR THE NES
Copyright ©2019-2022 by Steven Hugg

All rights reserved. No part of this book may be reproduced without written permission from the author.

Disclaimer
The publisher and author assume no responsibility for errors or omissions, nor is any liability assumed for damages resulting from the use of the information contained herein. No warranties of any kind are expressed or implied.

This book is an independent publication and is not associated with or endorsed by any party mentioned in this work.

Trademarks
NES® and Nintendo Entertainment System® are registered trademarks of Nintendo of America Inc. All trademarks in this work are the property of their respective owners. Use of a term in this work should not be regarded as affecting the validity of any trademark or service mark.

Inquiries
Please refer all inquiries to info@8bitworkshop.com.

Contents

1. The NES 1
   - 1.1 History 1
   - 1.2 Programming 4
2. The 8bitworkshop IDE 7
3. Quickstart 13
   - 3.1 Tweaking the Code 15
4. Binary Numbers 17
   - 4.1 Bits, Bytes, and Binary 17
   - 4.2 Hexadecimal Notation 18
   - 4.3 Signed vs. Unsigned Bytes 19
   - 4.4 Integer Overflow and Arithmetic 20
   - 4.5 Logical Operations 21
   - 4.6 Shift Operations 22
5. Memory Maps 23
   - 5.1 CPU Memory Map 23
   - 5.2 CPU vs. PPU Buses 24
6. The PPU 27
   - 6.1 The Video Signal 27
   - 6.2 PPU Address Space and Registers 29
   - 6.3 Pattern Table (CHR) 30
   - 6.4 Nametables and Background Layer 31
   - 6.5 System Colors 32
   - 6.6 Palettes 32
   - 6.7 Sprites and OAM 33

Contents

7 The Build Pipeline 35
    7.1   Support Libraries 35
    7.2   Preprocessor 36
    7.3   The C Compiler 37
    7.4   Linker 37
    7.5   Linking the Pattern Table 37

8 Nametables 39
    8.1   Setting the Palette 40
    8.2   Writing to Video RAM 40

9 Attribute Table 43
    9.1   Setting All of the Palettes 45
    9.2   Filling Up the Nametable 46
    9.3   Setting the Attribute Table 46

10 Scrolling 49
    10.1   Scrolling between Nametables 49
    10.2   put_str() function 51
    10.3   Writing to the Nametables 52
    10.4   Animated Scrolling 53
    10.5   NTSC vs PAL Animation Speed 55

11 Sprites 57
    11.1   OAM Buffer 57
    11.2   8x16 Sprites 59
    11.3   Setting Up the Palette and PPU 60
    11.4   Position and Velocity Arrays 61
    11.5   Drawing Sprites to OAM 63
    11.6   Performance 64

12 Metasprites 65
    12.1   Additional Metasprite Functions 67
    12.2   Flickering Sprites 68

13 Controllers 71
    13.1   Sprite Animation 73
    13.2   Trigger Mode 75

Contents

- 14 VRAM Buffer 77
  - 14.1 Using the VRAM Buffer Module 79

- 15 Split Status Bar 81
  - 15.1 Setting up Sprite Zero 82
  - 15.2 Vertical Mirroring 83
  - 15.3 Calling split() 83

- 16 Random Numbers 85
  - 16.1 The rand() function 85
  - 16.2 Entropy 86

- 17 Reading VRAM 87

- 18 PPU Mask Register 91

- 19 Virtual Bright 93

- 20 The APU 95
  - 20.1 Length Counter 98
  - 20.2 Examples 98

- 21 Simple Music 101
  - 21.1 Hitting the Right Note 101
  - 21.2 Laying out the Score 102
  - 21.3 Swinging with the Tempo 103
  - 21.4 Composing the Music 104

- 22 FamiTone Music 107
  - 22.1 FamiTone in C 108

- 23 Binary-Coded Decimals 111
  - 23.1 BCD Addition 112

- 24 RLE Encoding and Title Screens 115
  - 24.1 Compressing Nametables 116
  - 24.2 Other Techniques 118

- 25 Offscreen Scrolling 119
  - 25.1 Drawing Metatiles 121

- 25.2 Coloring Metatiles 123
- 25.3 Drawing Metatiles to the VRAM Buffer 123
- 25.4 Setting Attribute Blocks 124
- 25.5 The Main Loop 126
- 25.6 Alternate Methods 127

26 Main Loop vs. NMI Handler 129

27 Climber: Platform Game 131
- 27.1 Modeling The Game World 132
- 27.2 Generating The Game World 133
- 27.3 Drawing the Game World 134
- 27.4 Scrolling the Game World 138
- 27.5 Actors 140
- 27.6 The Player 141
- 27.7 Vanishing and Reappearing Actors 142
- 27.8 Drawing Actors 143
- 27.9 Scoreboard 145
- 27.10 Checking Collisions 145
- 27.11 The Main Game Loop 146
- 27.12 Level Win Animation 147
- 27.13 Music, Sound, and main() 147

28 Advanced Mappers 149
- 28.1 Cartridge Connector 149
- 28.2 Bank Switching 150
- 28.3 CHR ROM vs. CHR RAM 150
- 28.4 Extra or battery-backed RAM 150
- 28.5 Interrupts 151
- 28.6 Expansion Audio 151
- 28.7 Fast Multiplication 151
- 28.8 Advanced Mirroring 151

29 CHR RAM 153
- 29.1 Monochrome 1bpp Frame Buffer 154
- 29.2 Other CHR RAM Applications 158

30 Bank Switching 159
- 30.1 MMC3 Registers 161

	30.2	CHR ROM Switching and Other Features.......	163
31	IRQs	....	165
	31.1	MMC3 Interrupts	165
	31.2	Caveats..	167
32	Sprite Starfield...		169
33	The 6502 CPU		173
	33.1	The CPU and the Bus	173
	33.2	CPU Instructions	175
	33.3	Writing Loops	177
	33.4	Condition Flags and Branching.................	179
	33.5	Addition and Subtraction	181
	33.6	The Stack	182
	33.7	Logical Operations................................	183
	33.8	Shift Operations...................................	184
	33.9	Indirect Addressing	185
	33.10	Whew!..	186
34	Hello NES Assembly...		187
	34.1	Equates..	187
	34.2	Includes and Segments	188
	34.3	The iNES Header	189
	34.4	The NES_INIT Macro	191
	34.5	Warming up the PPU.............................	192
	34.6	Setting the Palette Colors.......................	194
	34.7	Enabling Rendering	194
	34.8	CPU Vectors and Interrupts.....................	195
35	Drawing Text in Assembly		197
	35.1	Setting the Palette	197
	35.2	Writing to the Nametable	199
	35.3	Linking the Pattern Table.......................	200
36	Scrolling in Assembly		201
	36.1	Filling up VRAM	201
	36.2	Scrolling in the NMI Routine	202

37	**Sprites/OAM in Assembly**	**205**
	37.1 Sprites	205
38	**Controller Reading in Assembly**	**209**
39	**FamiTone and DMC Samples**	**213**
	39.1 APU DMC Sound	213
40	**Split Screen X/Y Scrolling**	**215**
	40.1 VRAM Address Registers	216
	40.2 Setting Y Scroll During Rendering	217
41	**Line-by-line Scrolling**	**221**
	41.1 Scanline Manipulation	222
	41.2 A More Accurate Loop	225
42	**NES Dev Tools**	**227**
	42.1 8bitworkshop Asset Editor	227
	42.2 Other Tools	228
	42.3 Making Your Own Homebrew Game	229
Appendix A: NES Reference		**231**
Appendix B: NES Colors		**235**
Appendix C: NESLib Reference		**237**
Appendix D: C Library Reference		**239**
Appendix E: 6502 Instruction Flags		**241**
Appendix F: Powers of Two		**243**
Bibliography		**245**
Index		**247**

1

The NES

1.1 History

As Nintendo® game designer Gunpei Yokoi remembered it[1], the portable gaming revolution started with a boring ride on the Shinkansen bullet train and an unfortunate cold.

Nintendo President Hiroshi Yamauchi was scheduled to attend a meeting at the Plaza Hotel in Osaka, but his Cadillac driver was sick. Nintendo's HR manager frantically called Yokoi, an auto enthusiast and the only employee who could drive a car with a steering wheel on the left side.

Yokoi was not a chauffeur — he was the manager of Nintendo's Research and Development No. 1 Department. He decided to talk to Yamauchi about an idea that came to him on the train while he was watching a fellow commuter idly playing with buttons of his calculator:

> "I think it would be interesting to make a game machine like a small calculator. The conventional idea is to make games big and sell them for a high price, but if we make a system as thin and small as a calculator, even salarymen like us would play games."

He didn't think Yamauchi took him seriously, but before the Plaza meeting, the President of Sharp (the producer of the first

1. The NES

LCD calculator) sat next to Yamauchi and they discussed Yokoi's idea.

The next week, Yamauchi brought Sharp and Yokoi together and Yokoi began working on **Game & Watch** — kickstarting the portable gaming revolution.

The handheld systems sold like hotcakes, but the company would not produce a hit video game until 1981's *Donkey Kong*™. Masayuki Uemura was tasked with designing a game console, one with interchangeable cartridges that could faithfully recreate the arcade experience.

The personal computer boom had led to a shortage in microprocessors, so they looked to the manufacturer Ricoh to help produce custom chips for the new game console, guaranteeing them a three-million chip order. Ricoh suggested the 6502 CPU, which took up less chip space than the Z80.[2] It was selected for Nintendo's new console, dubbed the Family Computer, or **Famicom**.

Although the Famicom team suffered from defections to the revenue-positive Game & Watch team, their engineers would still contribute in important ways. One engineer, Katsuyah Nakawaka, took the controller Yokoi designed for the handheld version of *Donkey Kong* and hooked it up to the Famicom. It worked well, and this became the familiar *D-pad* configuration of the Famicom.[3] They also installed a 15-pin expansion port to the front of the console, allowing the optional use of an arcade-style joystick.

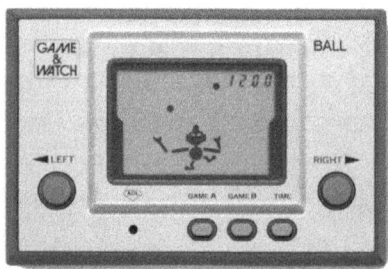

Figure 1.1: *The first Game & Watch product (CC BY-SA by ThePViana)*

1.1. History

The Famicom launched in Japan in July 1983. Despite a circuit defect that caused occasional system freezes prompting a recall of the first batch, the Famicom became a best seller in Japan: By the end of 1984, Nintendo sold more than 2.5 million consoles.

They then approached Atari to sell the Famicom in North America, but Atari's financial problems and their feelings of betrayal over Nintendo's licensing of *Donkey Kong* to competitor Coleco stalled the process.[4]

Nintendo decided to distribute the Famicom in the US themselves, but the release was complicated by the video game crash of 1983, which soured analysts and spooked retailers. To work around the "game console" stigma, Nintendo marketed the console as a full home computer in North America by changing its name to **Advanced Video System** (AVS) and adding a keyboard, cassette recorder, wireless controllers, and the BASIC programming language. After receiving a lukewarm reception, they went back to the drawing board.

The next iteration, branded the **NES** (Nintendo Entertainment System) was a Trojan horse of sorts. It would strip out the home computer elements, but to make it into retail stores, it had to disguise itself as something other than another video game console.

Instead of game cartridges, it would use "Game Paks," hidden inside of a front-loading chamber. The Zapper light gun and a disc-stacking "R.O.B." (Robotic Operating Buddy) generated a lot of buzz, and helped get reluctant toy retailers on board.

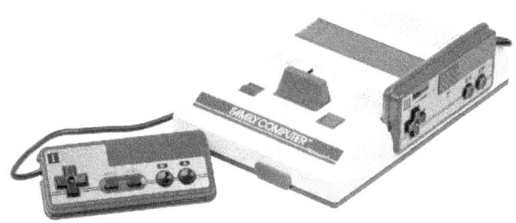

Figure 1.2: Family Computer ("Famicom") and controllers

1. The NES

A 90-day return policy sweetened the deal with retailers, and in October 1985, the NES launched in New York City bundled with both accessories and two games that used them: *Gyromite*™ and *Duck Hunt*®. For the nationwide release, Nintendo offered the "Action Set" which replaced the R.O.B. with *Super Mario Bros.*®

The company sold out of its inventory of 1.1 million consoles in 1986. The NES would dominate the home console market through the early 1990s.

1.2 Programming

Almost all NES commercial titles were written in 6502 *assembly* language. This allowed developers to fine-tune each and every byte of their programs. This was critical when fitting games into the small but expensive *ROM* in the game cartridge. It also allowed for clever optimizations which squeeze the most performance possible out of each frame of animation.

Since there was no "official" development kit, third-party developers hacked together their own, often using a custom cartridge attached via ribbon cable to a PC. Masahiro Sakurai revealed that, when working at for the game development company HAL Laboratory, they paired a Famicom console with the Famicom Disk System peripheral, and exclusively used a trackball to edit graphics and even enter code.[5]

Cartridges became more sophisticated over time. Studios expanded ROM sizes to as high as 512 KB, and included dedicated

Figure 1.3: Nintendo Entertainment System with controller

1.2. Programming

mapper chips to expand the console's functionality. Some games even included additional audio chips.

Nowadays, homebrew NES developers usually write games in either assembler or C, the latter using the **cc65** compiler toolchain. Writing in C gives you more functionality per line of code. While it has lower performance and greater code size than a well-written assembly program, you can still write a pretty good game in C.

The majority of this book will discuss code written in C using the **NESLib** library. We'll also write some 6502 assembly language, programming the NES hardware directly.

Figure 1.4: Cartridge for "NES Mission Control" development system, made by Rocket Science Production.

2

The 8bitworkshop IDE

In this chapter, we'll discuss the tools we'll use to develop and test our game code. These tools comprise our Interactive Development Environment, or *IDE*.

To start the **8bitworkshop IDE**, open https://8bitworkshop.com in your web browser and click **Continue to 8bitworkshop IDE**. For best results, use a recent version of Mozilla Firefox, Google Chrome, or Apple Safari.

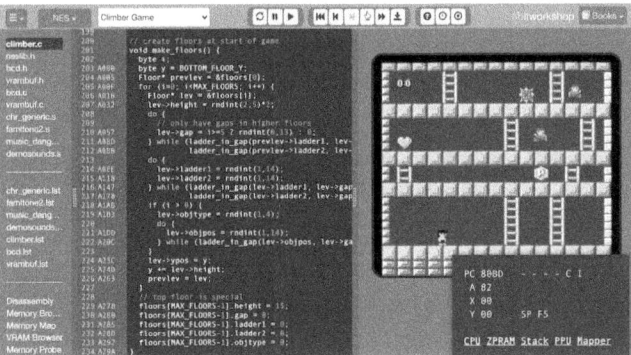

Figure 2.1: 8bitworkshop IDE

Once you've started the IDE, click the **Platforms** menu, then choose **Game Consoles » NES**, as seen in Figure 2.2.

2. The 8bitworkshop IDE

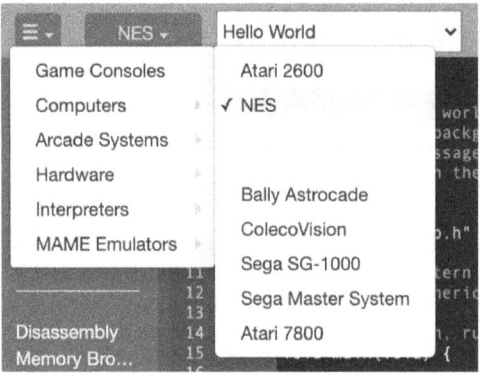

Figure 2.2: IDE platform menu

The IDE is packaged with several example programs. To the right of the menu icon, you can access a Project Selector drop-down menu that allows you to select a file to load, as shown in Figure 2.3.

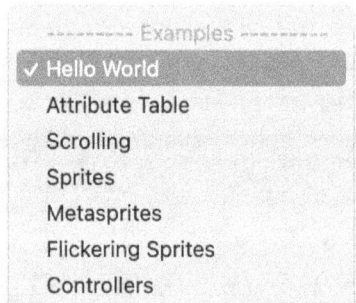

Figure 2.3: IDE Project Selector drop-down menu

You can edit these files as much as you want — all changes are persisted in browser local storage and they'll be there if you close the browser tab and come back. If you want to restore one of the example files back to its original condition, select **File » Revert to Original...** from the menu.

> Note that your changes will not be saved when using the browser's Incognito/Private browsing mode.

To start from scratch, select **New Project...** from the menu. Type in the name of your new file, typically with a `.c` extension for C source files. You can also write 6502 assembler with the `.dasm` or `.s` extension.

The IDE includes an NES *emulator* — we use **JSNES**[6], which runs the code on simulated hardware. To control the game, first click the emulator screen to gain focus. The keyboard commands are as follows:

Key	Function
Arrow Keys	Joypad
Z	B button
X	A button
Space	Select
Enter	Start

The IDE also includes a C compiler. The one we use is called **cc65**, and it also runs in the web browser, along with a web-based text editor. Each time you make a change to the code, it's immediately compiled and the ROM image is sent to the emulator, allowing you to see code changes near-instantly.

The last tool is a simple *debugger* that allows you to step through machine code instructions, view memory, and start and stop the program. The buttons at the top of the screen perform several debugging functions:

- **Reset:** Hard reset the emulator, then single-step to the first instruction.
- **Pause:** Stop the emulator.
- **Run:** Resume the emulator after pausing.
- **Step:** Execute the next CPU instruction, then break.
- **Next Frame/Interrupt:** Execute until the next video frame starts, then break.

- **Run To Line:** Set a *breakpoint* on the current line (the one the cursor is on). The emulator will stop when execution reaches that instruction.
- **Step Out of Subroutine:** Run until the current subroutine returns, then break.
- **Step Backwards:** Step back a single CPU instruction.

Whenever the IDE hits a breakpoint or is single-stepped, a debug window appears in the lower-right of the screen. This shows the internal state of the CPU, including all registers and flags. You can click the links at the bottom to see additional info.

PC 80C1 - - - - C I
A 00
X 00
Y 00 SP FB
CPU ZPRAM Stack PPU

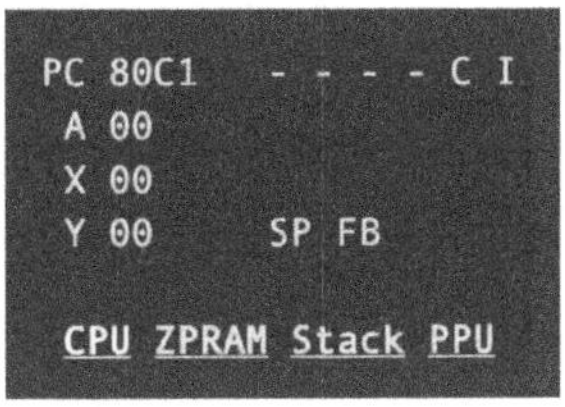

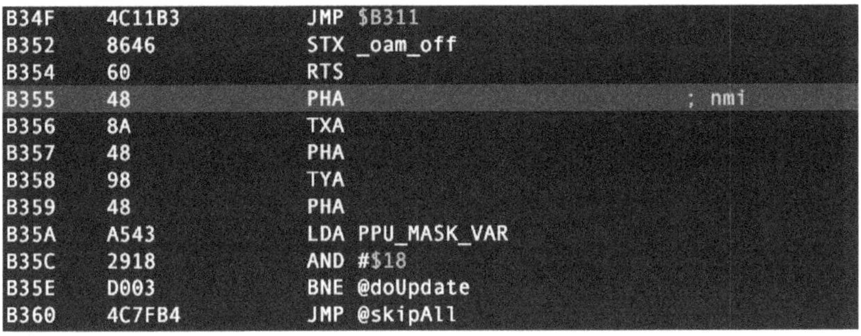

B34F 4C11B3 JMP $B311
B352 8646 STX _oam_off
B354 60 RTS
B355 48 PHA ; nmi
B356 8A TXA
B357 48 PHA
B358 98 TYA
B359 48 PHA
B35A A543 LDA PPU_MASK_VAR
B35C 2918 AND #$18
B35E D003 BNE @doUpdate
B360 4C7FB4 JMP @skipAll

Figure 2.4: Disassembler

If you want to save or share your work, you can choose **Sync** » **Publish Project on GitHub...** to upload your project to a new GitHub repository. You'll need to sign in to your GitHub account first.

You can also save your files to your local storage from the **Download** menu. Select **Download ROM Image** to download a binary ROM file of your project for use in other emulators.

> ℹ The IDE is under active development and may differ from what we describe here. The source code is available at `https://github.com/sehugg/8bitworkshop`.

3

Quickstart

To start programming as quickly as possible, we'll walk through a simple C program that displays text on the NES screen.

Most programming tutorials include a simple "Hello, World!" example, which prints a single line of text to the console. Usually this only takes a few lines of code, but on the NES, it's a little more complicated.

> ▶ Open the example on 8bitworkshop.com: From the **Platforms** menu, select **Game Consoles » NES**, then select the **Hello World** project from the Project Selector dropdown.

First, we include the **NESLib** header file. NESLib is a C library that gives us NES programming functions:

```
#include "neslib.h"
```

We also need to include a *pattern table*, which contains the bitmap graphics used by the game. The IDE includes a generic pattern table with letters and numbers.

We'll include it with a special #link command:

```
//#link "chr_generic.s"
```

3. Quickstart

When our game starts up, it runs the **main()** function. This, in turn, calls other functions which initialize the system and start our game.

```
void main(void) {
    ...
}
```

The first thing our main function will do is set the color of the entire screen. This is done with the **pal_col()** function:

```
pal_col(0,0x02);      // set screen to dark blue
```

We set it to hexadecimal 0x02, which translates into dark blue.

NES graphics are made out of 8x8 tiles. Each tile can have three different colors, chosen from a palette of 64 colors. Let's set the palette colors now:

```
pal_col(1,0x14);      // pink
pal_col(2,0x20);      // grey
pal_col(3,0x30);      // white
```

These tiles are arranged in a 32 column by 30 row grid called a *nametable*. The nametable chooses characters from the pattern table that go into a scrollable *background* layer.

To display our message, we need to put the bytes that comprise the text string HELLO, WORLD! into the nametable.

Writing to video memory requires two steps. First, we set the address to be written with the **vram_adr()** function.

```
vram_adr(NTADR_A(2,2));
```

NTADR_A is a C *macro* which calculates the *address* of a given column and row in a nametable. In our example, we've placed our HELLO, WORLD! on column two, line two.

Next, we call the **vram_write()** function, passing our HELLO, WORLD! string along with the number of bytes to write into video memory — 13 characters, in this case.

```
vram_write("HELLO, WORLD!", 13);
```

When our program starts, the screen is turned off. To display our text, we have to turn on the *Picture Processing Unit* (or *PPU*):

```
ppu_on_all();
```

We don't have anything else to do in this demo, so we enter an *infinite loop*:

```
while (1);
```

This keeps the CPU from exiting the *main()* function, which isn't allowed by our NES library — games are supposed to run forever, or at least until the console is reset.

The CPU will remain busy inside the infinite loop, but the PPU will continue to run, outputting frames of video to the emulated CRT. You should see the following message on the emulator screen:

3.1 Tweaking the Code

Now let's make a few changes to the example. Suppose we want the Hello, World! message to show up for just 10 seconds and then disappear.

To do this, we'll have to count video frames in a loop. We'll declare a *local variable* called x to hold the loop counter value.

Our C compiler requires us to declare all local variables at the beginning of a function, so we start by declaring x:

```
void main(void) {
    int x;                    // <-- add this line
```

3. Quickstart

We'll use a for loop to count from 0 to 499. Each loop iteration, we call **ppu_wait_frame()**. This function keeps the CPU busy until the next frame starts, which happens 50 times a second (more on this in Chapter 10).

```
for (x=0; x<500; x++) {     // <-- add these lines
    ppu_wait_frame();       // <-- after
}                           // <-- ppu_on_all()
```

After the loop ends, we call **ppu_off()** to turn the screen off:

```
ppu_off();                  // <-- add this line
```

We'll review this C example in more detail in Chapter 7. In the meantime, let's move onto reviewing some essential prerequisites for NES programming, starting with *binary* numbers.

> ▸ To revert your changes back to the original code, select **File** from the menu, choose **Revert to Original...** and click **OK** when prompted.

4

Binary Numbers

> If you're already familiar with binary and hexadecimal numbers, logical and shift operations, and unsigned vs. signed arithmetic, you can safely skip to the next chapter.

4.1 Bits, Bytes, and Binary

All digital computers operate on bits and bytes. Let's review a few things about them.

A *bit* is a binary value — it can be either zero (0) or one (1). We might also say it is off/on, or false/true. The important thing is that it can only have one of two values.

A *byte* is an ordered sequence of eight (8) bits. We say a computer has an *8-bit architecture* if it primarily manipulates bytes.

We can create a written representation of a byte in *binary* notation, which just lists the bits from left to right, for example: %00011011. We can then shorten the byte notation by removing the leading zeros, giving us %11011. (The % denotes a binary number.)

The eight bits in a byte are not just independent ones and zeros; they can also express numbers. We assign values to each bit and

4. Binary Numbers

then add them up. The least-significant bit, the rightmost (our index starts at zero, i.e., *bit 0*), has a value of 1. For each position to the left, the value increases by a power of two until we reach the most-significant bit, the leftmost (*bit 7*) with a value of 128.

Here are the values for an entire byte:

Bit #	7	6	5	4	3	2	1	0
Value	128	64	32	16	8	4	2	1

Let's line up our example byte, %11011, with these values:

Bit #	7	6	5	4	3	2	1	0
Value	128	64	32	16	8	4	2	1
Our Byte	0	0	0	1	1	0	1	1
Bit*Value				16	8		2	1

When we add up all the bit values, we get $16 + 8 + 2 + 1 = 27$.

A binary number with N bits has 2^N unique combinations, so an 8-bit number can represent 256 different values, including zero.

4.2 Hexadecimal Notation

Binary notation can be unwieldy, so it's common to represent bytes using *hexadecimal notation* – also known as *hex*, or more formally *base 16*.

We split the byte into two 4-bit halves, or *nibbles*. We treat each nibble as a separate value from 0 to 15, like this:

Bit #	7	6	5	4	3	2	1	0
Value	8	4	2	1	8	4	2	1

We then convert each 4-bit nibble's value to a symbol — 0-9 remains 0 through 9, but 10-15 becomes A through F.

Let's convert the binary number %11011 and see how it would be represented in hexadecimal:

Bit #	7	6	5	4	3	2	1	0
Value	8	4	2	1	8	4	2	1
Our Byte	0	0	0	1	1	0	1	1
Bit*Value				1	8		2	1
Decimal Value				1		11		
Hex Value				1		B		

We see in the above table that the decimal number 27, represented as %11011 in binary, becomes $1B in hexadecimal format.

It's easy to tell if a hex number is a *power of two* – the leftmost digit is 1, 2, 4, or 8, and the other digits are zeroes. For example, a *kilobyte* is equal to 2^{10} bytes (1024 in decimal, $400 in hexadecimal).

> The "$" prefix indicates a hexadecimal number in assembly language. In C programs, you'll see hex numbers prefixed by "0x", e.g., 0x1b or 0xAA. We'll use these two notations interchangeably in this book.

4.3 Signed vs. Unsigned Bytes

One more thing about bytes: We've described how they can be interpreted as any value from 0 through 255, or an *unsigned* value. We can also interpret them as negative or *signed* quantities.

This requires a trick known as *two's complement* arithmetic. If the high bit is 1 (in other words, if the unsigned value is 128 or greater), we treat the value as negative, as if we had subtracted 256 from it:

```
  0-127 ($00-$7F):    positive
128-255 ($80-$FF):    negative (value - 256)
```

Note that there's nothing in the byte identifying it as signed — it's all in how you interpret it, as we'll see later.

4.4 Integer Overflow and Arithmetic

Since the numbers we deal with in 8-bit CPUs are so small, *integer overflow* is a thing we'll have to deal with often.

When you add two numbers, the CPU adds them just like you would by hand, but in binary. Each binary digit is added, and if you have to carry the 1 (which only happens when adding the bits 1 and 1) you carry it to the next bit. An example:

Bit #		7	6	5	4	3	2	1	0
Byte A +		1	0	1	0	0	1	0	1
Byte B +		1	0	1	1	0	1	1	0
Carry	1		1			1			
=		0	1	0	1	1	0	1	1

Table 4.1: *Binary Addition of Two Bytes With Carry*

What happens to that extra carry bit? We only have 8 bits in a byte, so the result of the addition is *truncated* to 8 bits. We also could call this an *integer overflow*. The carry bit is retained in the CPU's Carry flag, and could be used by future calculations or just discarded.

An unsigned byte can only represent the values 0 to 255, so if $a + b >= 256$ then the 8-bit result is $(a + b)$ mod 256 (mod is the *modulo* operator, which is basically the remainder of a division.) For 16-bit unsigned numbers, it'd be $(a + b)$ mod 2^{16} (65536).

The overflow behavior actually makes integer subtractions work. The number -1 can be expressed as the signed byte $FF (255). The result of $a + 255$ is $(a + 255)$ mod 256, which is the same as adding -1 to a.

To visualize this, think of a wheel with 256 positions. Moving the wheel to the right by 255 positions is the same as moving it left by 1 position.

	254	255	0	1	2	Unsigned	126	127	128	129	130	
...	$FE	$FF	$00	$01	$02	....	$7E	$7F	$80	$81	$82	...
	-2	-1	0	1	2	Signed	126	127	-128	-127	-126	

Figure 4.1: *Signed vs. unsigned bytes.*

4.5 Logical Operations

Binary numbers support the logical operations AND, OR, and exclusive-OR (EOR or XOR). In C, the operators &, |, and ^ perform these operations.

AND only sets bits that are set in both arguments:

```
     $55  01010101
  &  $f0  11110000
  ---------------------
     $50  01010000
```

The AND operation is useful for limiting the range of a value. For example, AND #$1F is the same as (A mod 32) and the result will have a range of 0...31.

OR sets bits that are set in either argument:

```
     $55  01010101
  |  $f0  11110000
  ---------------------
     $f5  11110101
```

EOR (exclusive-or) is like an OR, except that bits that are set in both arguments are cleared.

```
     $55  01010101
  ^  $f0  11110000
  ---------------------
     $a5  10100101
```

If you do the same EOR twice, you'll get the original value back:

```
     $a5  10100101
  ^  $f0  11110000
  ---------------------
     $55  01010101
```

4. Binary Numbers

4.6 Shift Operations

We can also shift binary numbers left and right by a given number of bits. In C, the operators are left shift (<<) and right shift (>>).

Let's do a shift left by two bits, (0x17 << 2):

```
        $17  00010111    (23)
<< 2         -------------
        $5c  01011100    (92)
```

Just like decimal notation, we consider the leftmost bit to be the most significant. So if we shift left one bit, we are essentially multiplying by 2. In the above example, we shift left twice, multiplying by 4.

Now let's do a right-shift by two bits:

```
        $17  00010111    (23)
>> 2         -------------
        $05  00000101    (5)
```

If we shift right one bit, we essentially divide by 2. In the above example, we shift right twice, dividing by 4.

Note that the bits we shifted off the right side are *truncated* — i.e., they are thrown away. This effectively rounds down the division. Left-shifts are also truncated, which performs (A mod 256) when converting to an 8-bit value.

5

Memory Maps

5.1 CPU Memory Map

When the CPU loads or stores data, it uses an *address* to identify a location. We call the range of addresses it can access its *address space*.

There are several components connected to the CPU. Each component is responsible for handling read and write commands for a range of addresses. They are connected via common electrical signals, called a *bus*.

We organize these addresses into a *memory map* so that we can easily remember which addresses correspond to which component.

These components are connected to the NES CPU bus:

- **PRG RAM**: Memory that the CPU can read from and write to (modify).
- **PRG ROM**: The program code included on the game cartridge. The CPU can read this data, but can't write to it.
- **PPU** (*Picture Processing Unit*): Generates the video signal.
- **APU** (*Audio Processing Unit*): Generates audio.
- Additional components in the game cartridge, which may include extra RAM, ROM, or registers.

When programming the NES, we must be aware of where things are located in address space. "Where" means at which

5. Memory Maps

addresses. Due to its 16-bit address bus, there are 65,536 (2^{16}) possible addresses that the CPU can access.

Figure 5.1 provides an overview of this address space. Note that the addresses are given in hexadecimal, indicated by the $ prefix.

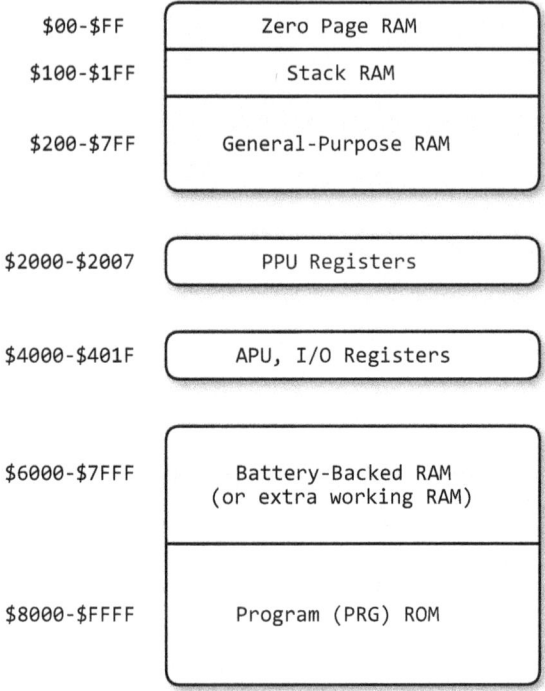

Figure 5.1: NES CPU Memory Map

5.2 CPU vs. PPU Buses

The CPU and PPU are connected via the main CPU bus. This is how the CPU commands the PPU to display video. But there is another independent bus which is controlled by the PPU.

The PPU bus is connected to the PPU's own *video RAM (VRAM)* and has its own separate memory map. The CPU cannot access the video RAM directly, but only through the PPU, and only under certain conditions.

5.2. CPU vs. PPU Buses

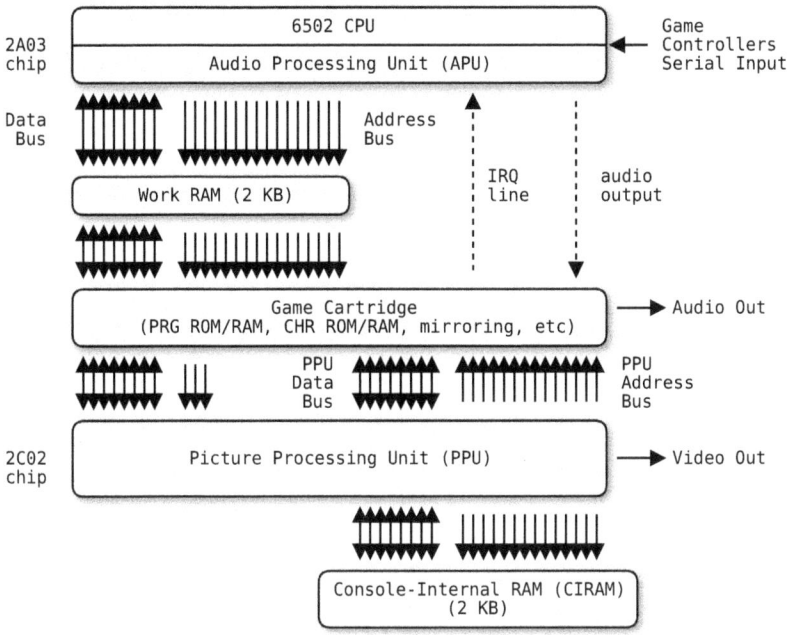

Figure 5.2: NES Bus Architecture

When generating video, the PPU reads its video RAM in a predictable pattern. You can think of the PPU as a little CPU that executes an internal program, the output of which is a video signal.

The CPU and PPU buses both go through the *cartridge connector*. This connects the cartridge's program (PRG) ROM to the CPU, and its graphics (CHR) ROM/RAM to the PPU.

The cartridge can do more than just serve up ROM data, however. By intercepting the signals via the cartridge connector, special hardware can expand the console's functionality. We call this special hardware a *mapper*. We'll discuss mappers later in the book.

6

The PPU

The NES's **PPU** (*Picture Processing Unit*) generates a *composite video signal* with 240 scanlines. This signal is compatible with the color television standards of the era: *NTSC* in Japan and the Americas, *PAL* in Europe.

Here are some quick PPU specifications:

- 256x240 visible resolution
- 64 colors (56 unique)
- 8x8 tiles, four colors per pixel (one transparent)
- 512 possible character patterns at one time
- 32x60 or 64x30 scrollable tile map in RAM
- 64 8x8 (or 8x16) sprites, up to eight sprites per scanline

6.1 The Video Signal

A *cathode ray tube* (*CRT*) has an electron beam that paints pixels from left-to-right, in horizontal lines called *scanlines*. The NTSC standard recommends 262.5 scanlines per frame, 60 frames per second. (We'll round that down to 262, because that extra half of a scanline relates to *interlacing*, which the NES doesn't do.)

6. The PPU

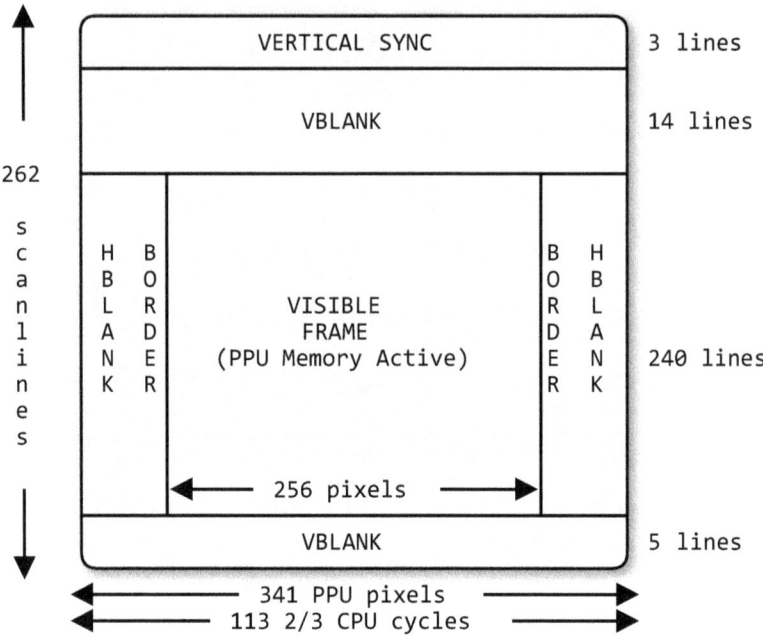

Figure 6.1: An NTSC-compliant video frame

The blank lines above and beneath the visible frame comprises the *vertical blank* period, or *VBLANK* — the period when the electron beam is turned off. This prevents the electron beam from being visible as it traces from the lower-right to the upper-left. The NES only displays visible pixels on 240 of the 262 total scanlines.

The three lines of *vertical sync* are essential. It's a special signal that tells the TV that a frame has ended and a new frame is beginning.

Each scanline counts a specific number of pixels horizontally. There are 341 total pixels in a scanline, but only 256 are visible on the NES. The other pixels are either blank, or *horizontal sync*, which tells the TV that a new scanline is starting.

A classic CRT exhibits *overscan* behavior: the visible signal goes beyond the extents of the frame. NES emulators replicate this behavior in different ways. To be on the safe side, assume the top and bottom 16 lines are cropped, as well as the leftmost and rightmost eight pixels.

6.2 PPU Address Space and Registers

The CPU cannot read from or write to the PPU's address space directly. The PPU has its own address space, which includes internal RAM on the console and external ROM (or RAM) on the cartridge.

The CPU interacts with the PPU by writing to (or reading from) various *registers*. These registers enable and disable video features, control scrolling, and read and write PPU memory.

When using assembler, you'd read and write certain locations in memory to access these registers. (See Appendix A: NES Reference for details.) In C, we will usually rely on library functions to manipulate the registers.

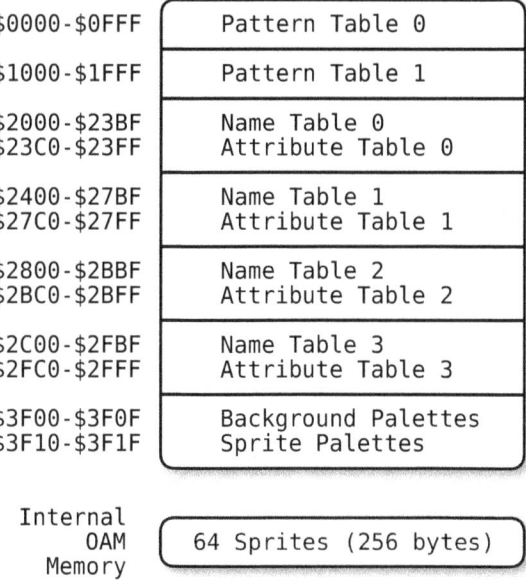

Figure 6.2: PPU internal memory map

6. The PPU

6.3 Pattern Table (CHR)

The *pattern table* is an area of memory connected to the PPU that defines tile graphics for a game. It's stored on the cartridge, usually as immutable ROM data, but sometimes as RAM.

A pattern table stores bitmap data for 256 tiles, each eight pixels wide by eight pixels high. There's room for two pattern tables at once — usually, the first table is for background tiles, and the second table is for sprites.

Each tile in the pattern table takes up 16 bytes, split into two *bitplanes* of eight bytes each. The PPU combines these two bitplanes so that each pixel has two bits — four possible values per pixel.

A zero indicates a transparent pixel, which shows through to the background screen color. The other three values choose a color from one of four *palette*s.

Figure 6.3: Pattern table with 256 tiles (4096 bytes)

6.4. Nametables and Background Layer

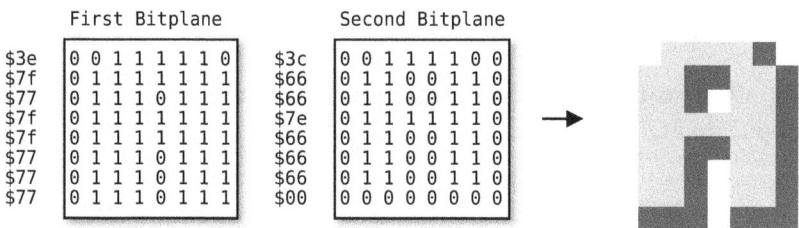

Figure 6.4: Combining two bitplanes to make a four-color tile

6.4 Nametables and Background Layer

The PPU renders a grid of tiles called the *background* layer. It can be used for title screens, status bars, and scrolling worlds, among other things.

A *nametable* is defined by a 32 column by 30 row array of bytes. Each nametable generates a 256 pixel wide by 240 pixels high image — an entire screen of tiles.

Each byte in the nametable chooses one of 256 tiles from the pattern table. For example, the byte $03 chooses the fourth tile in the background pattern table.

There's enough RAM in the NES for two complete nametables. But the address space covers four nametables, which allows horizontal or vertical scrolling, as we'll see in Chapter 10.

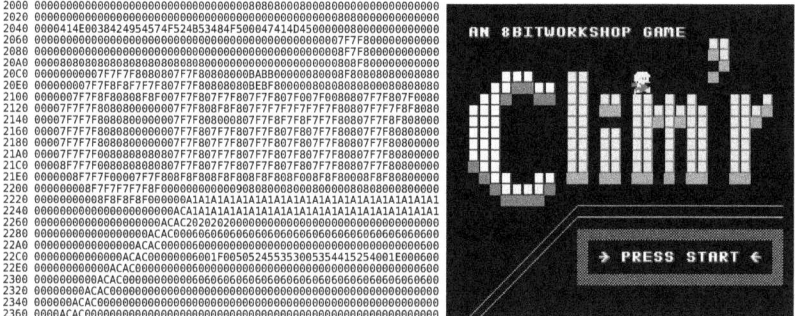

Figure 6.5: Nametable layout

6. The PPU

6.5 System Colors

The NES can generate 64 different color values, though only about 56 are unique.[1]

+	0	1	2	3	4	5	6	7	8	9	a	b	c	d	e	f
0x00																
0x10																
0x20																
0x30																

The NES system palette is organized in four rows of sixteen. Each successive row moves up a level of brightness, or *luminance*. Columns 0 and 13 contain shades of grey, and columns 1 through 12 contain various hues. The two rightmost columns are all black, except entry 13 ($0D) which is a blacker-than-black color that can interfere with the video signal.

6.6 Palettes

The NES can't display every color from the system palette at the same time. The four *background palettes* and four *sprite palettes* determine which colors can be used. The former controls nametable colors, while the latter controls sprite colors.

Each palette has three bytes, each byte indexing a color in the system palette. There is also a single byte which controls the *screen color*, which shows though when no background or sprite pixel is present.

Screen Color	03		
Background 0	11	30	27
Background 1	1C	20	2C
Background 2	00	10	20
Background 3	06	16	26
Sprite 0	16	35	24
Sprite 1	00	37	25
Sprite 2	0D	2D	3A
Sprite 3	0D	27	2A

Each nametable has an associated *attribute table* which determines the palettes used by tiles. We'll cover attribute tables in Chapter 9.

---

[1] You can find a table of color names in Appendix B: NES Colors.

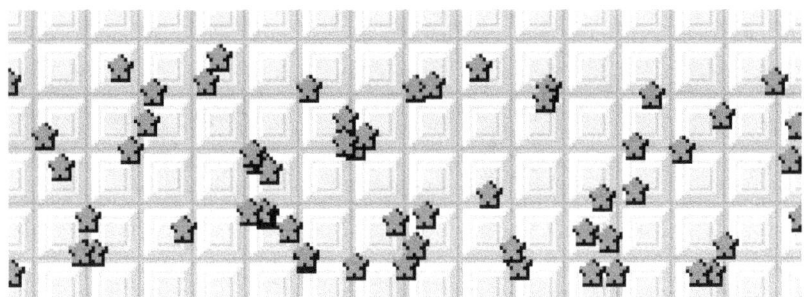

Figure 6.6: 64 8x8 sprites overlapping a tiled background.

6.7 Sprites and OAM

The PPU can draw up to 64 sprites. They allow a game to render fast-moving objects on top of (or behind) the background layer.

Sprites can be placed at any coordinate on the screen. Each sprite can display one of 256 tiles in a pattern table, and can take one of four palettes. Sprites can also be flipped horizontally and vertically.

The PPU can be set so that each sprite is a single tile (8x8 pixels) or two tiles stacked vertically (8x16 pixels).

The sprites' positions and attributes aren't kept in regular video memory. They live in *OAM* (Object Attribute Memory), a 256-byte memory space inside of the PPU. We'll cover sprites in more detail in Chapter 11.

7

The Build Pipeline

Since this book is about programming to the hardware's bare metal, we're going to dissect the code we wrote in Chapter 3 all the way down to the bytes of the machine code.

First, let's talk about the C compiler *pipeline*: the several steps that are needed to turn your source code into a final ROM image that is loaded into the machine.

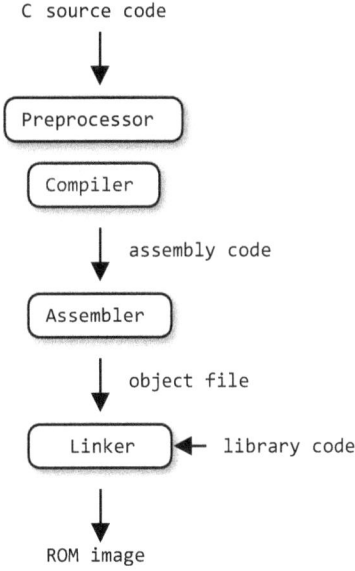

Figure 7.1: C Compiler Pipeline

7.1 Support Libraries

The **cc65** compiler includes its own set of libraries, which support the C *runtime* — basic language functions, like pushing and popping function parameters onto the stack, moving memory, and integer math. It also includes a C-compatible *standard library*, which provides some helpful functions for handling memory and strings.

7. The Build Pipeline

For NES-specific support, we use **NESLib**[7], created by Alex 'Shiru' Semenov. It helpfully interfaces with the **cc65** compiler, and provides a low-level set of functions for graphics and sound. The IDE automatically links in NESLib and the cc65 built-in libraries.

> ▸ Open the example on 8bitworkshop.com: From the **Platforms** menu, select **Game Consoles » NES**, then select the **Hello World** project from the Project Selector dropdown.

7.2 Preprocessor

The first line is a *preprocessor directive*, indicated by a hash (#) at the start of the line:

```
#include "neslib.h"
```

The *preprocessor* is the first thing that touches the C source code. One of its primary jobs is to include *header files* into the source, which contain various C declarations and macro definitions.

The above #include directive tells the preprocessor to include the text of the header file **neslib.h** into the code. This imports all of the NESLib declarations into our source file.

Your C code (or included files) can contain *macro* definitions, which tell the preprocessor to substitute one string for another, with optional parameters. It's common to use these for constant values, for example:

```
#define EXTRA_LIFE_SCORE 10000
```

You can also use them for complex expressions, code generation, and all sorts of other mischief. We'll cover some practical uses of macros later on.

7.3 The C Compiler

When the C compiler compiles a source file, it produces an *assembly* file as output. This file contains 6502 instructions to be executed by the CPU. The **ca65** *assembler* then translates these instructions into *object files*.

Here's an excerpt of the *listing file* which shows the assembled instructions for each source file (you can see the complete listing file by clicking hello.lst on the left side of the IDE):

```
000028r 1                    ; vram_adr(NTADR_A(2,2));
000028r 1                    ;
000028r 1                            .dbg    line, "hello.c", 23
000028r 1   A2 20             ldx     #$20
00002Ar 1   A9 42             lda     #$42
00002Cr 1   20 rr rr          jsr     _vram_adr
```

7.4 Linker

After assembly, the *linker* combines the produced object file(s) with startup code, support libraries, and pattern table (*CHR ROM*) data. The result is a final ROM image that can be loaded into an emulator.

You may have noticed various "r"s in the listing file above. This indicates *relocatable* code, data that does not yet have an absolute address in memory. The linker is responsible for converting all these "r"s into absolute addresses as it composes the various object files into the final ROM.

7.5 Linking the Pattern Table

Every NES program that displays graphics requires a *pattern table*, the set of 8x8 tile bitmaps used for background and sprites. We're using *CHR ROM*, so we have to include this data into our final ROM file.

We have to tell the *linker* to include our pattern table. We use a special directive that only works in the **8bitworkshop IDE** (outside the IDE, if you were compiling on the command line,

7. The Build Pipeline

you'd link the pattern table file in your build script). It's actually a C "//" comment, but the 8bitworkshop IDE recognizes it as a *link directive*:

```
//#link "chr_generic.s"
```

The **chr_generic.s** file doesn't contain any assembly code. It just contains a single 4096-byte array which defines the pattern table. We put the data into the CHARS segment so that the linker knows to place it at the end of the ROM file:

```
.segment "CHARS"
.byte $00,$00,$00,$00,$00,$00,$00,$00
; ... continues to 4096 bytes of data ...
```

You can see (and edit) this character map by clicking the **Asset Editor** link on the left side of the IDE.

> Click the **Reset** button in the IDE, then click **Disassembly** on the left side toolbar to see the 6502 instructions in the ROM. Note that the cursor is positioned right after address $8000, which is where the NESLib initialization code starts.
>
> Click **Memory Map** to see the entire NES address space. You can click any of the segments to view it in the **Memory Browser**. When we start defining global variables, the DATA segment will display them.

8

Nametables

Our first C example will simply display the text HELLO, WORLD! on an emulated NES screen. We'll do this by writing the characters to the nametable, then turning on the PPU.

> Open the example on 8bitworkshop.com: From the
> **Platforms** menu, select **Game Consoles** » **NES**, then
> select the **Hello World** project from the Project Selector
> dropdown.

We're going to define a function called **main()**, which is traditionally the first code to run when a C program starts:

`void main (void) {`

The first void is the *return type* of the function — our **main()** function doesn't return a value, so its type is void.

8. Nametables

Our function doesn't take any parameters, so we make this explicit by putting void in the parameter list. (In practice, you can omit the second void.)

> In C, all identifiers must begin with a letter or underscore. Subsequent characters may also contain the digits 0-9. Upper and lower case are distinct.

8.1 Setting the Palette

Our demo will set the palette colors before setting up the PPU. We'll write the screen color, which is palette index 0. Then we'll write three more values, which sets colors for the first background palette.

We'll call the NESLib function **pal_col()** to set the palette colors:

```
pal_col(0,0x02);      // set screen to dark blue
pal_col(1,0x14);      // fuchsia
pal_col(2,0x20);      // grey
pal_col(3,0x30);      // white
```

Each function call passes two arguments. The first argument is the palette entry index, and the second is the color value.

These function calls don't set the PPU directly, but instead update *shadow registers* in RAM. During the next *NMI (vertical blank interrupt)*, i.e., the start of the next video frame, NESLib will copy them to the PPU. This allows the program to modify palette colors at any time without worrying about whether the PPU is active or inactive.

8.2 Writing to Video RAM

To write text to the screen, we have to write to video RAM, which is controlled by the PPU. The PPU is turned off when the **main()** function starts, so we can write to video memory without getting in its way.

8.2. Writing to Video RAM

First, we have to figure out the address in the nametable where we want to start writing text. NESLib provides the NTADR_A macro to do this.

This macro takes X (column) and Y (row) coordinates and computes the corresponding position in the nametable. There are macros for nametables A, B, C, and D — but we're just using nametable A in this example. Here's how it's defined in **NESLib.h**:

```
#define NAMETABLE_A    0x2000
#define NTADR_A(x,y)   (NAMETABLE_A|(((y)<<5)|(x)))
```

The NTADR_A macro shifts the y argument left by 5 bits, effectively multiplying it by 32, which is the length of a nametable row in bytes. It bitwise-ORs the result with the x argument and the constant 0x2000, producing the final nametable address.

> Macros modify source code before it gets to the compiler. If both the x and y arguments to the macro are constants, then the compiler will reduce the entire expression to a constant, which improves code size and speed. For example, NTADR_A(2,2) reduces to 0x2042.

The next two lines write to video RAM:

```
vram_adr(NTADR_A(2,2));           // set address
vram_write("HELLO, WORLD!", 13);  // write bytes to PPU
```

The first line calls the NESLib function **vram_adr()** with the result of our NTADR_A macro. Behind the scenes, it'll write the 16-bit address we calculated to the PPU_ADDR register. This sets the video RAM address in the PPU, which we'll use in the next step.

The next line calls **vram_write()**, which writes multiple bytes to the PPU_DATA register. The first argument is a pointer to the data; in this case, it's a string of characters.

The second argument to **vram_write()** is the number of bytes to write: 13, the number of characters in "HELLO, WORLD!"

8. Nametables

Now that we've set up the nametable and palette, it's time to turn rendering back on in the PPU, which enables video output:

```
ppu_on_all();
```

Then we create an infinite loop. A **while** statement repeats as long as the condition in parentheses is non-zero. Thus, the CPU will never exit this loop:

```
while (1) ;
```

The PPU will merrily and perpetually output the video frame we've defined.

> Try changing the colors in this examples. See *Appendix B: NES Colors* on page 235 for a full list of NES-supported colors.
>
> Also try changing the text string. What happens if you write more than 32 bytes at once?

9

Attribute Table

In the last chapter, we wrote to the nametable to draw text in the background layer. So far, we've been limited to a single palette, limiting us to three colors for the entire screen.

If we want different areas of the screen to use different color palettes, we can write to the *attribute table*. Each nametable has a corresponding attribute table, and it allows us to pick four different palettes for background tiles.

The attribute table doesn't address individual tiles — it operates on 2x2 blocks of tiles, 16x16 pixels square. Each block can be assigned one of four different palettes.

> ▶ Open the example on 8bitworkshop.com: From the **Platforms** menu, select **Game Consoles** » **NES**, then select the **Attribute Table** project from the Project Selector dropdown.

Figure 9.1: Four different palettes for a background tile

9. Attribute Table

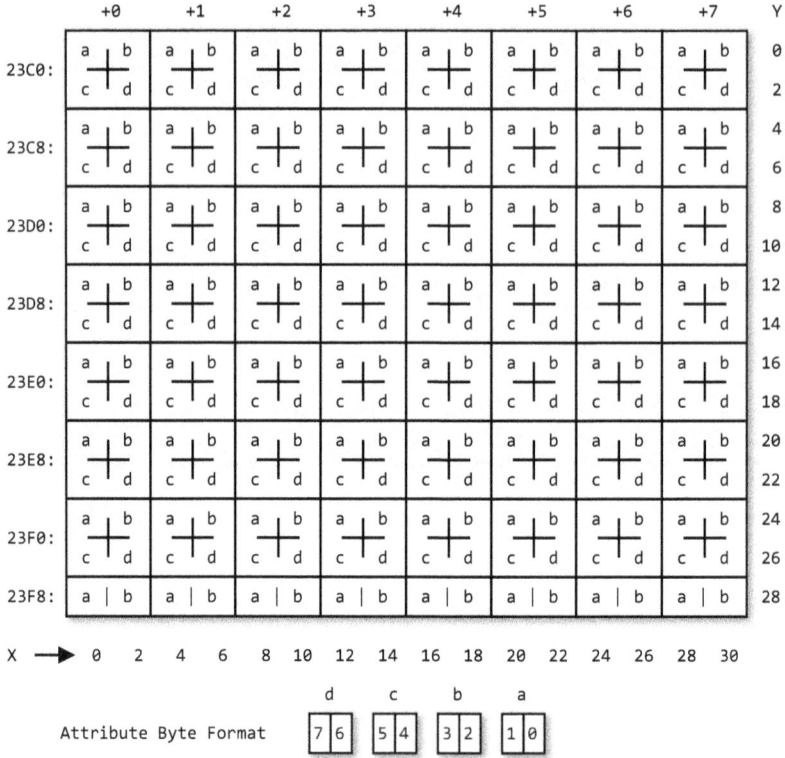

Figure 9.2: Attribute table layout

An attribute table is only 64 bytes long, located in memory directly following its nametable. It defines a 16x15 grid that covers the same screen area as the nametable, as shown in Figure 9.2.[1]

Each byte in the attribute table contains four entries, each entry covering a 2x2 quadrant of a 4x4 block of tiles.

Each attribute table entry is two bits long, defining a value from 0 to 3. This value selects one of four background palettes. This palette is applied to a 2x2 tile block in the nametable.

---

[1] Since nametables are only 30 rows high, the last row of the attribute table is cut in half.

9.1 Setting All of the Palettes

We're going to configure the attribute table to use all four palettes, so we'll need to set their colors.

Instead of setting them one-by-one with **pal_col()**, we'll set them all at once, placing the palette values into a 16-byte *const* byte array:

```
// define an array of 16 bytes in ROM
const char PALETTE[16] = {
  0x03,                  // screen color
  0x11,0x30,0x27,0x0,    // background palette 0
  0x1c,0x20,0x2c,0x0,    // background palette 1
  0x00,0x10,0x20,0x0,    // background palette 2
  0x06,0x16,0x26         // background palette 3
};
```

> The **const** keyword indicates that these variables are constant; i.e., they will never change. The compiler stores them directly in the ROM file. If we had omitted the **const** keyword, they would also be copied into RAM, which is a waste of storage.

> The array elements are type **char**, an *unsigned* 8-bit integer data type in our compiler. We could have also used **byte**.

In our **main()** function, we set all of the background palette entries with a single call to **pal_bg()**:

```
pal_bg(PALETTE);
```

This passes a pointer to the start of the PALETTE array to the **pal_bg()** function, which then sets the palette *shadow register*s all at once. They'll be copied to the PPU during the next vertical blank.

9. Attribute Table

9.2 Filling Up the Nametable

We also want to fill the nametable with a pattern in order to demonstrate the attribute table's varied colors. We'll choose tile 0x16, which in our pattern table is a diamond shape.

We'll use **vram_adr()** to set the PPU address, then **vram_fill()** to write the byte 0x16 to the PPU 960 times:

```
vram_adr(NAMETABLE_A);        // start address ($2000)
vram_fill(0x16, 32*30);       // fill nametable (960 bytes)
```

9.3 Setting the Attribute Table

We will copy the entire attribute table from ROM. We've defined 64 bytes of attribute table data in a *const* array, just like we did for the palette:

```
// attribute table in PRG ROM
const char ATTRIBUTE_TABLE[0x40] = {
  0x00, 0x00, 0x00, 0x00, 0x00, 0x00, 0x00, 0x00, // rows 0-3
  0x55, 0x55, 0x55, 0x55, 0x55, 0x55, 0x55, 0x55, // rows 4-7
  0xaa, 0xaa, 0xaa, 0xaa, 0xaa, 0xaa, 0xaa, 0xaa, // rows 8-11
  0xff, 0xff, 0xff, 0xff, 0xff, 0xff, 0xff, 0xff, // rows 12-15
  0x00, 0x01, 0x02, 0x03, 0x04, 0x05, 0x06, 0x07, // rows 16-19
  0x08, 0x09, 0x0a, 0x0b, 0x0c, 0x0d, 0x0e, 0x0f, // rows 20-23
  0x10, 0x11, 0x12, 0x13, 0x14, 0x15, 0x16, 0x17, // rows 24-27
  0x18, 0x19, 0x1a, 0x1b, 0x1c, 0x1d, 0x1e, 0x1f  // rows 28-29
};
```

We can copy this array to the attribute table with **vram_adr()** and **vram_write()**:

```
vram_adr(NAMETABLE_A + 0x3c0);   // 0x23c0
vram_write(ATTRIBUTE_TABLE, sizeof(ATTRIBUTE_TABLE));
```

> The **sizeof** keyword is a C operator that evaluates to the size in bytes of an array or other data type. Here, it returns 0x40 (64 bytes).

9.3. Setting the Attribute Table

When we write a byte to the PPU, its internal PPU address pointer advances by one. After the call to **vram_fill()**, the PPU address will have advanced 960 (0x3c0) times. Thus it will point to the beginning of the attribute table, which directly follows the nametable (see Figure 6.2 on page 29). Because of this, we can omit the **vram_adr()** in this example.

In our example, we copied an entire attribute table directly from PRG ROM. There may be times when you want to modify attribute table entries individually — for example, when drawing tiles offscreen for a scrolling level. We'll do this in Chapter 25. In Chapter 24, we'll decompress a full title screen into VRAM, including both the nametable and attribute table.

> Try changing the colors by modifying values in the PALETTE array. You can also use the **Asset Editor**.
>
> You can alter the shape used to fill the screen by changing the 0x16 constant in the call to vram_fill. Hover the cursor over tiles in the **Asset Editor** to choose a value.
>
> You can also edit the values in the ATTRIBUTE_TABLE array. Can you make a checkerboard pattern of different colors?

10

Scrolling

To make the game world appear larger than a single screen, we can use the NES's scrolling features.

So far, we've only been using a single nametable that takes up the entire screen. If we use multiple nametables, we can scroll the screen between them. Due to the limited RAM available in the system, however, we're working with a few limitations.

10.1 Scrolling between Nametables

The NES has four logical nametables — we'll call them A, B, C, and D — arranged in quadrants:

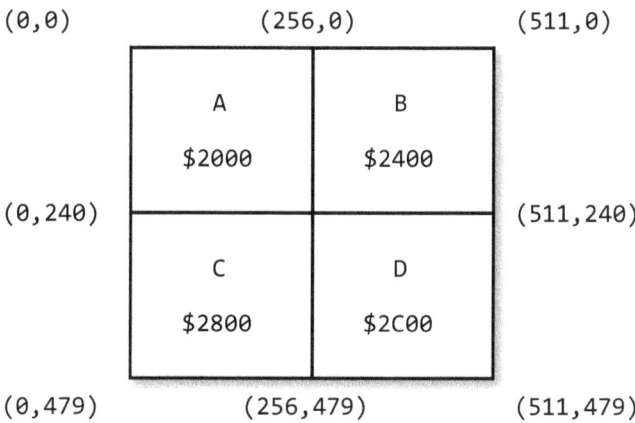

Figure 10.1: The four logical nametables

10. Scrolling

The NES only has enough built-in RAM (2 KB, 2048 bytes) for two nametables. A *mirroring* scheme can map these two physical nametables into the four logical nametables. There are several schemes you can use, the choice of which largely depend on the type of scrolling in the game. In this chapter, we'll talk about horizontal and vertical mirroring schemes.

Basically, we're sliding around a 256x240 pixel window in a 512x480 area, made up of four nametables. There's only enough RAM to store tile data for two nametables, but a *mirroring* scheme duplicates the other two.

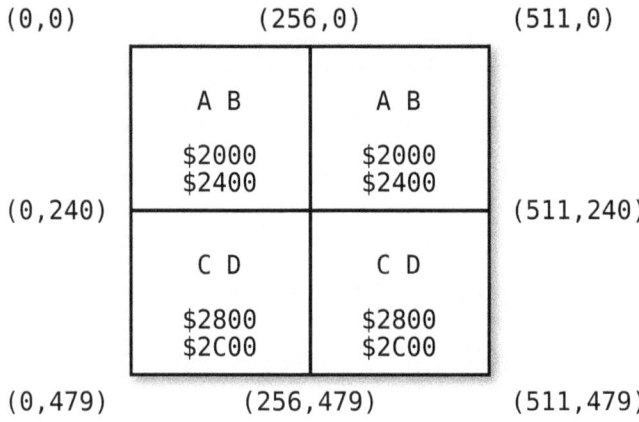

Figure 10.2: Horizontal mirroring.

If we map nametables A and B to the first half of nametable RAM, and nametables C and D to the second half, we get the arrangement shown above. This is called *horizontal mirroring*, the default setting for our examples.

Horizontal mirroring is used for games that scroll vertically, because you have two unique nametables stacked on top of each other. You can update one nametable offscreen without affecting the other.

But it's not as useful for scrolling horizontally, because there's only one screen's worth of data in that direction, and you'll just wrap it around and around.

10.2. put_str() function

```
   (0,0)           (256,0)          (511,0)
          ┌─────────────┬─────────────┐
          │    A C      │    B D      │
          │             │             │
          │   $2000     │   $2400     │
          │   $2800     │   $2C00     │
   (0,240)├─────────────┼─────────────┤(511,240)
          │    A C      │    B D      │
          │             │             │
          │   $2000     │   $2400     │
          │   $2800     │   $2C00     │
          └─────────────┴─────────────┘
   (0,479)         (256,479)        (511,479)
```

Figure 10.3: Vertical mirroring.

If we share the RAM for nametables A and C, and for B and D, we get the arrangement shown above. Here, we have two unique nametables side-by-side. This is called *vertical mirroring*, and it's used for games that scroll horizontally, with or without a status bar.

Now, let's apply our knowledge and make a vertically scrolling display.

 Open the example on 8bitworkshop.com: From the **Platforms** menu, select **Game Consoles** » **NES**, then select the **Scrolling** project from the Project Selector dropdown.

10.2 put_str() function

In our "Hello, World!" example, we used two lines of code to write a string to video RAM. To make writing text to the screen easier, we'll create a new *function* to do the same thing using a single line.

Our function will need to compute the length of a string using the **strlen()** function. It's declared in the C standard library header file **string.h**, which we'll include in our code like so:

```
#include <string.h>
```

10. Scrolling

Our function, which we'll call **put_str()**, will need to know which nametable to write the string to, the string's horizontal and vertical positions, and the string itself.

We'll declare this function before the **main()** function begins, making it usable within **main()** or from any other function:

```
void put_str(unsigned int adr, const char *str) {
  vram_adr(adr);              // set PPU read/write address
  vram_write(str, strlen(str)); // write bytes to PPU
}
```

Note that instead of specifically defining the string length the way we did for Hello, World! we use the **strlen()** function to calculate the size of the string for us.

10.3 Writing to the Nametables

Now, inside the **main()** function, let's use the **put_str()** function to print some text to video RAM. (We'll skip over the background palette-setting, as it's the same as in the previous example.)

We'll write text to nametables A (top-left) and C (bottom-left) using the following lines:

```
put_str(NTADR_A(2,0),  "Nametable A, Line 0");
put_str(NTADR_A(2,15), "Nametable A, Line 15");
put_str(NTADR_A(2,29), "Nametable A, Line 29");
put_str(NTADR_C(2,0),  "Nametable C, Line 0");
put_str(NTADR_C(2,15), "Nametable C, Line 15");
put_str(NTADR_C(2,29), "Nametable C, Line 29");
```

You can see how this text is arranged in Figure 10.4.

10.4. Animated Scrolling

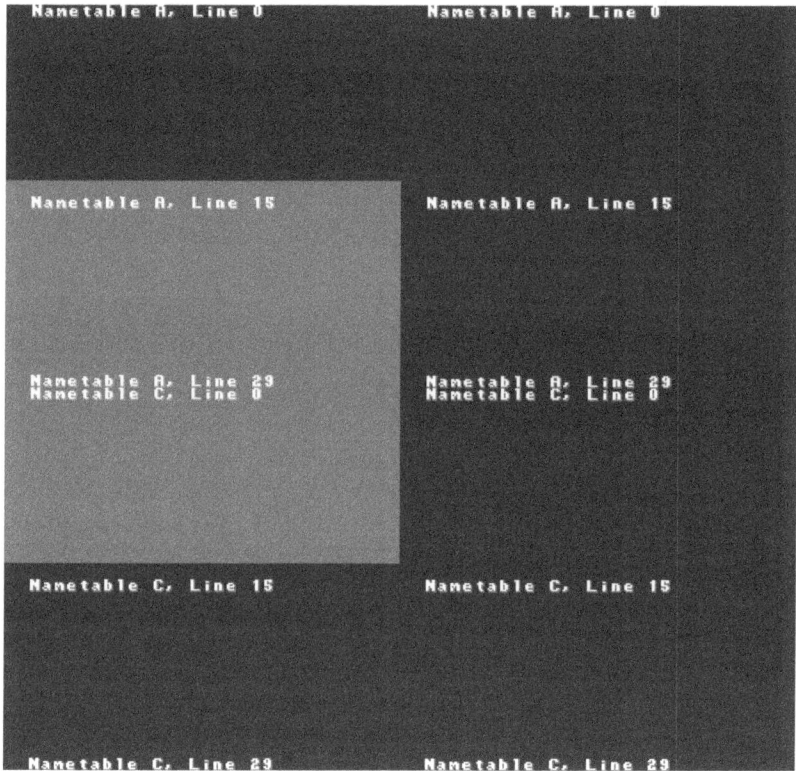

Figure 10.4: The content of the four logical nametables (A, B, C, and D). The highlighted square shows the size of the visible region. Note that the left and right sides are mirrored.

10.4 Animated Scrolling

Next, we'll add another global function (also above **main()**) named **scroll_demo()** that perpetually scrolls the playfield up and down. We'll begin by declaring *local variable*s for scroll position and direction:

```
// function to scroll window up and down until end
void scroll_demo() {
  int x = 0;   // x scroll position
  int y = 0;   // y scroll position
  int dy = 1;  // y scroll direction
```

10. Scrolling

> In C, *local variables* (those declared within a function) are stored on the stack. The 6502 stack is only 256 bytes at most, so the **cc65** compiler uses a separate stack for function parameters and local variables. Generally, *global variables* (those declared outside of any function) generate smaller and faster code, but take up permanent space in RAM.

After these variables are defined, we start an infinite loop using the **while** keyword:

```
// infinite loop
while (1) {
```

Within this loop, for each iteration, we call **ppu_wait_frame()** to wait for the next video frame:

```
ppu_wait_frame();
```

Now we update the Y scroll position, and change direction (dy) when we have scrolled two full nametables, a total of 480 scanlines:

```
// update y variable
y += dy;
// change direction when hitting either edge of scroll area
if (y >= 479) dy = -1;
if (y == 0) dy = 1;
```

We used **if** statements to see if the y variable is greater or equal to 479, or if it is equal to zero. In both cases, we reverse dy, reversing the direction of the scroll.

Finally, the **scroll()** function sets the X and Y scroll positions:

```
scroll(x, y);
```

> It's common in computer graphics for X to represent horizontal coordinates from left to right, and Y to represent vertical coordinates from top to bottom.

scroll() doesn't change things immediately, but actually sets *shadow register*s which will be applied to the PPU during the next *vertical blank*. This prevents glitches that would appear if the registers were changed while a frame was being drawn. (Though sometimes you do want to set the PPU registers directly, as we'll see later.)

Note that the **scroll()** function takes 16-bit arguments, although only the first 9 bits are used. So any value above 512 is wrapped around to 0. Since two side-by-side nametables are exactly 512 pixels wide, scrolling horizontally is no problem. When scrolling vertically, you must ensure the Y position is less than 480 or the scrolling will appear to jump.

Now let's turn on the PPU and start scrolling by adding these functions to **main()**:

```
ppu_on_all();
scroll_demo();
```

10.5 NTSC vs PAL Animation Speed

To ensure that games running on *PAL* (50 Hz) and *NTSC* (60 Hz) run at the same speed, there are two different **ppu_wait** functions.

When using NTSC mode, **ppu_wait_frame()** slows it down by waiting one extra frame every five frames so that the game runs at 50 Hz. Therefore, if you call the function 50 times, it will always take one second in either mode.

ppu_wait_nmi() waits until the next video frame, whether in PAL or NTSC mode. So calling this function 60 times takes one second in NTSC, and 1.2 seconds in PAL.

Regardless, after exiting either **ppu_wait** function, the PPU will have just started *vertical blank*.

▶ In this demo, we only modify the Y scroll position. Can you make the X scroll position bounce left and right?

11

Sprites

In a typical game, the background layer displays the game world, and moving objects are displayed using *sprites*.

The PPU can render up to 64 sprites. Each sprite is eight pixels wide by eight (or 16) pixels high.

Unlike the background tiles, sprites can be positioned independently of each other, anywhere on the screen. They can be drawn either on top or underneath the background, with zero-value pixels behaving as transparent.

You can have no more than eight sprites on a single scanline. If you have more than eight, some sprites will be partially or completely missing when running on actual hardware.

11.1 OAM Buffer

The sprite data is held in 256 bytes of RAM inside the PPU called *OAM* (Object Attribute Memory). The PPU can fill OAM by reading directly from the CPU's RAM, usually once per video frame.

11. Sprites

Each sprite is defined by four bytes in OAM:

Byte Offset	Description
0	Y coordinate
1	Tile index in pattern table
2	Attributes (palette, priority, X/Y flip)
3	X coordinate

Table 11.1: OAM Sprite Structure

Tile index, byte 1: This byte determines which tile in the pattern table to draw. Just like the nametable, it selects one of 256 tiles.

Y coordinate, byte 0: This is the scanline above the top of the sprite. The sprite will start drawing on the next line. You can hide a sprite below the visible screen by writing a value of `$EF` (239) or above.

X coordinate, byte 3: The horizontal position of the sprite, 0 being the left edge. Values of `$F9-$FF` (249-255) result in the right side of the sprite partially displayed offscreen.

While you can't position a sprite partially off of the left side of the screen, you *can* set `PPU_MASK` to mask (or blank out) the left eight pixels, and then position sprites there.

Note: In the emulator, the top eight and left eight pixels are masked since they are often not visible on CRT displays. So a sprite at coordinate (8,7) would appear flush against the upper-left corner of the emulator screen.

Attributes, byte 2: This byte selects one of four sprite palettes, independent of the four background palettes. In addition, other bit flags available allow you to place the sprite in front of or behind the background, and flip the sprite horizontally and vertically.

Bit Index	Hex Mask	C Expression	Description
0-1	0x3	*integer*	Palette select (0-3)
5	0x20	OAM_BEHIND	Sprite under background (priority)
6	0x40	OAM_FLIP_H	Flip pixels horizontally
7	0x80	OAM_FLIP_V	Flip pixels vertically

Table 11.2: Sprite Attribute Bits

The priority bit only affects a sprite's relation to the background layer. The position of a sprite in OAM determines whether it overlaps other sprites. Sprites with a lower index in OAM (i.e., added first) will overlap sprites with a higher index (i.e., added later).

Figure 11.1: Sprite priority: The top eight sprites have the priority flag OAM_BEHIND set, putting them behind the background tiles.

11.2 8x16 Sprites

Sprites have dimensions of either 8x8 or 8x16 pixels — this is a global setting in the PPU_CTRL register that applies to all sprites on the screen.

If 8x16 sprites are selected, tiles from both pattern tables are available for sprites.

- **8x8 Mode**: This selects a tile in the pattern table from 0-255, or if bit 3 of PPU_CTRL is set, a tile from 256-511.
- **8x16 Mode**: Two consecutive tiles are selected, the first for the top half and the second for the bottom half. If bit 0 is set, it adds 256 to the pattern index instead of 1. So the ordering goes: 0, 256, 2, 258, 4, 260, etc.

The sprites and background can use the same or different pattern tables. In 8x8 Mode, you can use the **bank_spr()** function to choose either the first (0-255) or second (256-511) pattern table for sprite data. The **bank_bg()** does a similar selection for the background.

11. SPRITES

11.3 Setting Up the Palette and PPU

> Open the example on 8bitworkshop.com: From the **Platforms** menu, select **Game Consoles » NES**, then select the **Sprites** project from the Project Selector dropdown.

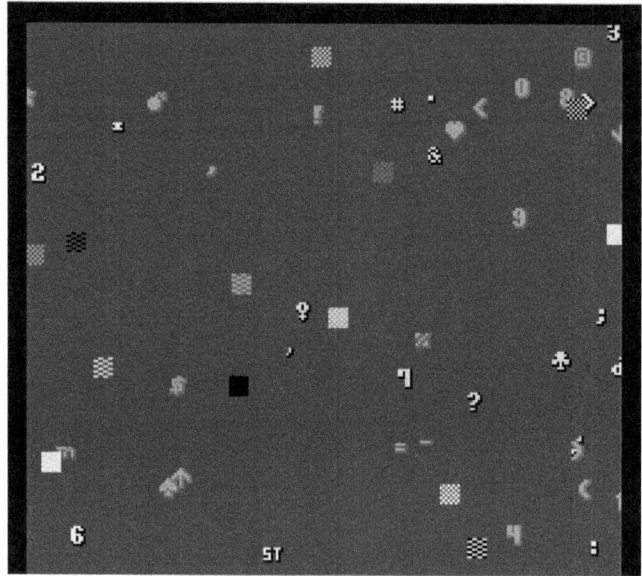

Figure 11.2: Demo with 64 8x8 sprites

In this example, we'll animate all 64 hardware sprites. First, we need to set the *sprite palette*.

In the first example, we set palette colors individually using the **pal_col()** function. Then we used the **pal_bg()** function to set all of the background palettes.

This time, we'll use the **pal_all()** function to set all entries of the background and sprite palettes at once. We'll define a 32-byte const array to hold all of these color entries.

```
/*{pal:"nes",layout:"nes"}*/
const char PALETTE[32] = {
  0x03,                     // screen color
  0x11,0x30,0x27,0x0,       // background palette 0
  0x1c,0x20,0x2c,0x0,       // background palette 1
  0x00,0x10,0x20,0x0,       // background palette 2
  0x06,0x16,0x26,0x0,       // background palette 3
  0x16,0x35,0x24,0x0,       // sprite palette 0
  0x00,0x37,0x25,0x0,       // sprite palette 1
  0x0d,0x2d,0x3a,0x0,       // sprite palette 2
  0x0d,0x27,0x2a            // sprite palette 3
};
```

> You can view and edit the palette by clicking the **Asset Editor** link on the left side of the IDE. When you change a color in the Asset Editor, the palette code will automatically change within your C file.

For convenience, we create a function to set up the PPU. We'll do this in three steps.

First, we call **oam_clear()** which places all 64 hardware sprites offscreen, effectively hiding them. Next, we send the entire palette to PPU using **pal_all()**. Finally, we turn on the PPU using **ppu_on_all()**:

```
void setup_graphics() {
  oam_clear();              // hide all sprites
  pal_all(PALETTE);         // set palette colors
  ppu_on_all();             // turn on PPU
}
```

11.4 Position and Velocity Arrays

We use a *preprocessor define* to set the maximum number of sprites, which we call *actors* here. In this example, one actor is equal to one hardware sprite. We'll use all 64 available sprites:

```
#define NUM_ACTORS 64       // 64 sprites (maximum)
```

11. Sprites

Now we define arrays for the X/Y positions of each actor. Each array is 64 bytes long.

```
byte actor_x[NUM_ACTORS];    // horizontal coordinates
byte actor_y[NUM_ACTORS];    // vertical coordinates
```

We also have arrays for the *delta*, or change to the X/Y coordinate. These values will be added to the X/Y positions once per frame. They can be negative, so we define them as type sbyte, or *signed* byte:

```
sbyte actor_dx[NUM_ACTORS];   // horizontal velocity
sbyte actor_dy[NUM_ACTORS];   // vertical velocity
```

Now we're ready to start working on our **main()** function by declaring some local variables:

```
void main() {
  byte i;          // actor index
  byte oam_id;     // sprite ID
```

The oam_id variable tracks the current offset into the *OAM buffer*. The first sprite is 0. Since each sprite takes up four bytes, the second sprite is 4, the third sprite is 8, and so on.

Next, we'll initialize the sprite arrays with random values:

```
  for (i=0; i<NUM_ACTORS; i++) {
    actor_x[i] = rand();
    actor_y[i] = rand();
    actor_dx[i] = (rand() & 7) - 3;
    actor_dy[i] = (rand() & 7) - 3;
  }
```

We included the **stdlib.h** header file to access the standard C **rand()** function. It gives us a 16-bit random number, with a range of 0 to 65,535. Since we're storing them into arrays of bytes, they'll be truncated to eight bits, for a final range of 0 to 255.

For the actor_dx and actor_dy arrays, we want smaller numbers. The & operator (bitwise-AND) forces the result of **rand()** to be between 0 and 7, then we subtract 3. So the final result has a range of -3 to 4.

11.5 Drawing Sprites to OAM

First we call our **setup_graphics()** function to initialize the PPU:

```
setup_graphics();
```

Our animation code will be wrapped in an infinite **while** loop:

```
while (1) {
}
```

We're going to start with the first sprite, so we set oam_id to 0:

```
// start with OAMid/sprite 0
oam_id = 0;
```

Now we use the **for** keyword to loop through the indices of all actors, 0 through 63:

```
// draw and move all actors
for (i=0; i<NUM_ACTORS; i++) {
```

To draw a sprite, we call **oam_spr()** to write sprite data into the OAM buffer. This function takes five parameters:

- X coordinate
- Y coordinate
- Tile to use for the sprite from our linked pattern table
- Sprite attributes (palette, priority, vertical/horizontal flip as described in Table 11.2)
- The index in the OAM buffer where the sprite data should be copied (oam_id).

So, we'll call **oam_spr()** the following way:

```
oam_id = oam_spr(actor_x[i], actor_y[i], i, i, oam_id);
```

The **oam_spr()** function takes oam_id as a parameter, and also returns oam_id. This sets up for the next sprite by adding four to the current oam_id index.

Note that we're passing i for both the pattern and attribute parameters. This gives the sprites a variety of colors and orientations, which is fine for a quick demo. For example, if you wanted instead to use diamond shapes and sprite palette 2, you'd do this:

```
oam_id = oam_spr(actor_x[i], actor_y[i], 0x16, 0x02, oam_id);
```

We also update the X/Y positions of each actor, using the += operator to add each dx/dy array element to the x/y arrays:

```
actor_x[i] += actor_dx[i];
actor_y[i] += actor_dy[i];
```

After we're done drawing sprites, we call **oam_hide_rest()**. This erases the rest of the sprites in the 64-sprite array.

One warning though: If oam_id has wrapped around to zero, this function call will erase all sprites. So we check oam_id first, calling **oam_hide_rest()** only if it is non-zero:

```
if (oam_id != 0) oam_hide_rest(oam_id);
```

We then make sure to call **ppu_wait_frame()** once per loop:

```
ppu_wait_frame();
```

You should see 64 sprites flying happily around the screen.

11.6 Performance

If you go frame-by-frame in the emulator (using the **Next Frame** button on the toolbar) you'll see that not all sprites move during each frame. This is because the code for updating all 64 sprites takes longer than a single frame. The overhead of C and of the **oam_spr()** function are significant, taking about five scanlines to update and move a single sprite.

In the next chapter we'll use *metasprite*s to update several hardware sprites with a single C function, allowing for larger objects.

 Can you make the sprites go faster? Slower? In different directions? What if you reduce the NUM_ACTORS value?

12

Metasprites

The NES hardware sprites are pretty small by gaming standards. If we're limited to 8x8 or 8x16 sprites, how do we make larger moving objects?

We use *metasprite*s — larger sprites made by stitching together several hardware sprites. For example, a 16x16 pixel metasprite can be built from four 8x8 hardware sprites. You can arrange these sprites in arbitrary ways, even overlapping sprites within the metasprite.

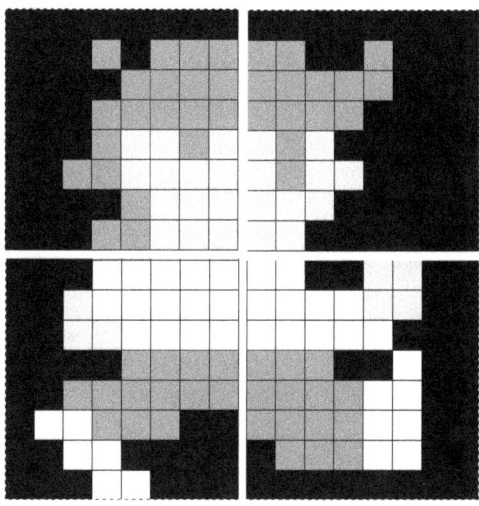

Figure 12.1: 16x16 metasprite layout, using four 8x8 sprites

12. METASPRITES

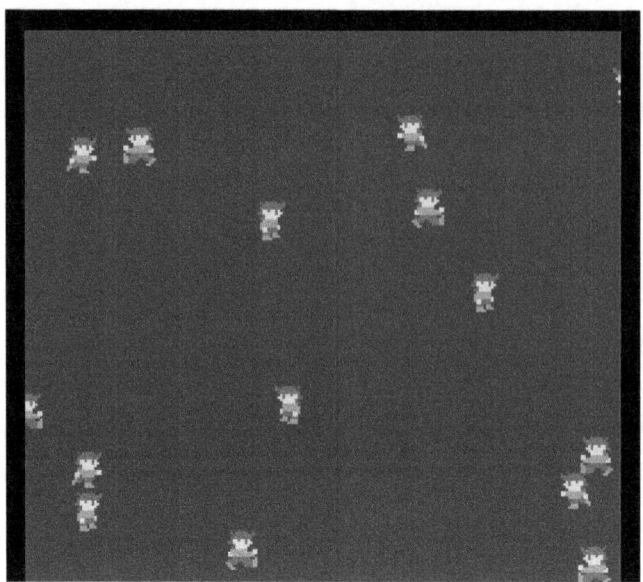

Figure 12.2: Demo with sixteen 16x16 metasprites, each consisting of four 8x8 sprites

NESLib requires a specific data structure to define a metasprite. Each four-byte entry defines an individual sprite.

The first two bytes are the X and Y offsets from the origin of the metasprite. The next two bytes are the tile index and attributes (palette, priority, flip). The constant "128" marks the end of the metasprite definition.

```
const unsigned char metasprite[]={
  <x offset>, <y offset>, <tile>, <attribute> of 1st sprite
  <x offset>, <y offset>, <tile>, <attribute> of 2nd sprite
  ...
  128    // end of metasprite marker
};
```

> Open the example on 8bitworkshop.com: From the **Platforms** menu, select **Game Consoles » NES**, then select the **Metasprites** project from the Project Selector dropdown.

For example, a 16x16 metasprite using a grid of four hardware sprites looks like this:

```
const unsigned char metasprite[]={
    0,    0,    TILE+0,   ATTR,    // upper-left
    0,    8,    TILE+1,   ATTR,    // lower-left
    8,    0,    TILE+2,   ATTR,    // upper-right
    8,    8,    TILE+3,   ATTR,    // lower-right
    128};                          // end of definition
```

TILE and ATTR are *macros* we've defined to make things a bit easier to change:

```
#define TILE 0xd8
#define ATTR 0x00
```

The **setup_graphics()** function is just the same as in the previous chapter, so we won't repeat it here.

Also like the previous chapter, we define the number of actors as NUM_ACTORS. We'll set it to 16, because each metasprite uses 4 hardware sprites, therefore our 16 metasprites will use all available 64 hardware sprites.

The rest of the **main()** function is identical to what we used in the **sprites.c** example, except for our sprite drawing function. To draw metasprites, we use the **oam_meta_spr()** function:

```
oam_id = oam_meta_spr(actor_x[i], actor_y[i], oam_id,
    metasprite);
```

Be careful of the eight sprite-per-line restriction, as it's easy to hit the limit since metasprites result in lots of hardware sprites near each other. (Note: The **JSNES** emulator used in the **8bitworkshop IDE** uses does not model this hardware limitation as of this writing.)

12.1 Additional Metasprite Functions

NESLib provides some additional functions to make things easier.

oam_meta_spr_pal() draws a metasprite but allows you to change the attribute byte for each hardware sprite. It's useful

12. Metasprites

for changing the palette and sprite priority. It's less useful for creating a flipped version of a metasprite — we'll see how to do that in Chapter 13.

oam_meta_spr_clip() is for larger metasprites. It omits hardware sprites that are outside of the screen area.

Neither of these functions pass or return the oam_id parameter. Instead, they implicitly use the global zero-page variable oam_off to track the sprite offset in the same way.

You should initialize the oam_off variable before using these functions in a given frame, for example:

```
oam_off = 0;
oam_meta_spr_pal(x, y, pal, meta);   // adds 4 to oam_off
```

12.2 Flickering Sprites

If we have more moving objects than will map to the 64 hardware sprites, we could use *sprite shuffling* techniques. This means we'll only show a subset of the objects on each frame to create a flickering effect.

 Open the example on 8bitworkshop.com: From the **Platforms** menu, select **Game Consoles** » **NES**, then select the **Flickering Sprites** project from the Project Selector dropdown.

We'll set NUM_ACTORS to 24, which is eight more than we can draw, since each actor uses four hardware sprites.

We have to fairly rotate the sprites so that no object is left out for more than a frame or two. So we'll just draw sprites until we run out of OAM, and then pick up where we left off in the next frame, using the same counter index.

We'll use **oam_meta_spr_pal()** to draw the metasprites, so we'll first set the oam_off variable to zero. We'll exit our **while** loop when oam_off is 240 or greater, which means we only have room for four more hardware sprites.

12.2. Flickering Sprites

```
oam_off = 0;
// draw and move all actors
// (note we don't reset i each loop iteration)
while (oam_off < 256-4*4) {
  // advance and wrap around actor array
  if (++i >= NUM_ACTORS)
    i -= NUM_ACTORS;
  // draw and move actor
  oam_meta_spr_pal(
    actor_x[i] += actor_dx[i],  // add x+dx and pass param
    actor_y[i] += actor_dy[i],  // add y+dy and pass param
    i&3,                         // palette color
    metasprite);                 // metasprites
}
```

Note that we've moved the instructions that update the X/Y positions (using the += operator) into the function call parameters! These expressions modify the array first, and then return the result. Most modern C compilers think this is silly, but CC65 is so old school that doing it this way makes the code a bit faster.

Since we know we haven't overflowed oam_id past 255, we don't have to check it before calling **oam_hide_rest()**:

```
oam_hide_rest(oam_off);
```

To wait for the next frame, we call **ppu_wait_nmi()**. This is because **ppu_wait_frame()** would skip every sixth frame on NTSC, which would make the flickering look worse.

There are many other schemes for sprite shuffling, depending on your goals. One improvement is limiting the number of sprites on a scanline to eight or less. If your sprites are evenly distributed, an easy way to do this would be to draw the left half of the screen in one frame, and the right half of the screen in the next frame.

By the way, this code has a small bug. It doesn't even handle when the number of actors is less than the number of sprites — it might draw (and move) sprites multiple times! (Try setting NUM_ACTORS to 4, you'll see what I mean.)

12. Metasprites

> These examples use 8x8 sprites. The pattern table we're using has the right layout to also support 8x16 sprites.
>
> Can you modify the Metasprites example to use 8x16 sprites? You'll have to change the metasprite definitions and call the **oam_size(1)** to use just two side-by-side sprites. By default, oam_size is set to 0 for 8x8 sprites, so you must explicitly set **oam_size(1)** in the code to use 8x16 sprites.

13

Controllers

Each NES controller has eight buttons (or "switches").

Each switch can be mapped to a bit in a byte, so that 1 is "pressed" and 0 is "not pressed." There are eight switches, so the controller state fits into a single byte:

Bit index	7	6	5	4	3	2	1	0
Switch	Right	Left	Down	Up	Start	Select	B	A

The NES reads controller data via *serial* port, one bit at a time. Reading the controllers in assembly code via the I/O port is a little involved, so we'll save it for later. NESLib makes it easy to read controllers in C without worrying about all that stuff.

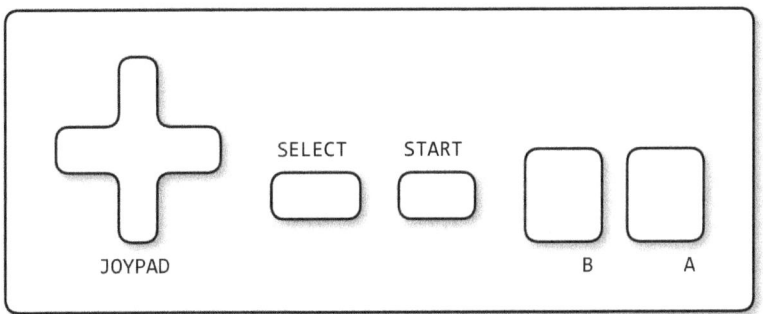

Figure 13.1: NES controller switch layout

13. CONTROLLERS

> ▸ Open the example on 8bitworkshop.com: From the **Platforms** menu, select **Game Consoles » NES**, then select the **Controllers** project from the Project Selector dropdown.

You can poll the left controller (0) or the right controller (1) using **pad_poll()**:

```
// poll controller i (0-1)
pad = pad_poll(i);
```

There are several PAD_xxx constants in NESLib that let you test the controller state using an AND mask. Let's use these to move a metasprite around the screen.

To move left and right, we first poll the controller state. We then bitwise-AND (&) the result of **pad_poll()** against PAD_LEFT and PAD_RIGHT.

We can use **if** statements to test these conditions, chained together by the **else** keyword. This code might look like this:

```
if (pad & PAD_LEFT) actor_dx[i]=-2;
else if (pad & PAD_RIGHT) actor_dx[i]=2;
else actor_dx[i]=0;
```

> In C, a zero value is *false*, and any non-zero value is *true*. So these if statements only succeed if the result of their AND expression is non-zero, which only happens if the desired bit is set.

We'd like to also prevent the player from going off the side of the screen. So we'll do a boundary check on the metasprite's position. We'll only allow it to go left if the X coordinate is greater than zero.

13.1. Sprite Animation

Similarly, we'll only allow it to go right if the X coordinate is lower than 232:

```
if (pad&PAD_LEFT && actor_x[i]>0) actor_dx[i]=-2;
else if (pad&PAD_RIGHT && actor_x[i]<232) actor_dx[i]=2;
else actor_dx[i]=0;
```

Moving up and down is similar, using `PAD_UP` and `PAD_DOWN`:

```
if (pad&PAD_UP && actor_y[i]>0) actor_dy[i]=-2;
else if (pad&PAD_DOWN && actor_y[i]<212) actor_dy[i]=2;
else actor_dy[i]=0;
```

 What happens if you remove the boundary checks in the code?

13.1 Sprite Animation

Our demo shows a little person flying around the screen. To make our person walk, climb, and jump, we'll have to cycle between several different metasprites.

The code for defining a metasprite is a little verbose. We can define a macro to make it more succinct.

The macro will define a 16x16 pixel metasprite in the form we saw in the previous chapter, using four consecutive tiles in the pattern table. We just pass the identifier name, starting tile index, and palette/attributes to the macro:

```
#define DEF_METASPRITE_2x2(name,code,pal)\
const unsigned char name[]={\
  0,    0,    (code)+0,   pal, \
  0,    8,    (code)+1,   pal, \
  8,    0,    (code)+2,   pal, \
  8,    8,    (code)+3,   pal, \
  128};
```

For example, to declare a metasprite named `playerRStand` starting at tile index `0xd8` with an attribute byte of 0:

```
DEF_METASPRITE_2x2(playerRStand, 0xd8, 0);
```

13. Controllers

This metasprite shows the player standing to the right. To flip the metasprite to the left, we'll have to rearrange the sprites and set the horizontal flip flag in the attributes. We've got a different macro that we'll use to define left-facing metasprites:

```
DEF_METASPRITE_2x2_FLIP(playerLStand, 0xd8, 0);
```

We also want to animate the person while it's running. We can put metasprites into an array, like so:

```
const unsigned char* const playerRunSeq[16] = {
        playerLRun1, playerLRun2, playerLRun3,
        playerLRun1, playerLRun2, playerLRun3,
        playerLRun1, playerLRun2,
        playerRRun1, playerRRun2, playerRRun3,
        playerRRun1, playerRRun2, playerRRun3,
        playerRRun1, playerRRun2,
};
```

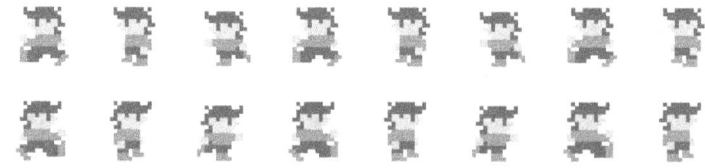

Figure 13.2: Array of 16 metasprites for running animation.

Note that the array contains eight left-facing sprites, then eight right-facing sprites. This makes the math easier. We just have to AND the X coordinate with 7, putting it into the range 0 to 7. Then, if the player is standing or moving to the right, we add 8 to the index, putting it into the range of right-facing metasprites:

```
  byte runseq = actor_x[i] & 7;    // animation index
  if (actor_dx[i] >= 0)            // moving to right?
    runseq += 8;                   // add 8 to index
```

Note that when the player stops, they face to the right, even if they were moving left. We can fix this by using a persistent flag for the player's direction. The platform game we'll create in Chapter 27 will do this and much more.

13.2 Trigger Mode

Trigger mode is an additional NESLib feature for reading controllers. It can be convenient when you want to read a single button press or single joypad movement, for example when navigating a menu.

pad_trigger() will only return inputs the first time a switch is pressed — subsequent calls will return 0 for these switches until they're released.

```
pad = pad_trigger(i); // read controller i in trigger mode
```

Reading from a controller takes the CPU a few scanlines to complete — that is, the PPU will have drawn a few scanlines by the time the function call returns.

So try not to call both **pad_trigger()** and **pad_poll()** if you want a combination of triggered and polled inputs. Instead, you can call **pad_state()** to get the last known state of a controller's inputs:

```
pad = pad_trigger(i); // takes several scanlines to complete
pad = pad_state(i);   // returns previous value
```

> ▶ Can you make the player run faster while the B button is pressed? When going up and down, how about a climbing animation using `playerLClimb` and `playerRClimb`?

14

VRAM Buffer

We've seen how to write data to video RAM using the **vram_adr()** and **vram_write()** functions. However, these only work when the PPU is inactive.

Sometimes, we want to modify the background layer while the game is running. This is often used in games with worlds that are larger than the available nametable RAM.

We can't write to video RAM while the PPU is busy drawing the screen. We have to either turn the PPU off (disabling the display) or wait for the *vertical blank* period before writing to video RAM.

We want to do as many updates as possible during the short vertical blank period. So while the PPU is active, we'll fill up a *VRAM buffer* with a list of commands. When the NMI handler runs, it reads the commands and copies data from CPU RAM to video RAM as quickly as possible.

NESLib expects a specific format for the VRAM buffer, composed of a series of packets. Each packet starts with the 16-bit VRAM address, then is followed by either a byte or a series of bytes.

To write a single byte to VRAM, a three-byte packet is required:

```
Byte 0: [VRAM address hi byte]
Byte 1: [VRAM address lo byte]
Byte 2: [data byte]
```

14. VRAM Buffer

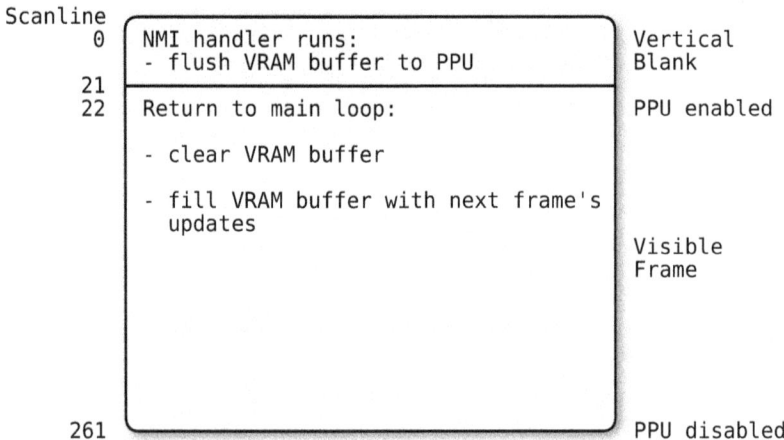

Figure 14.1: Using VRAM buffer during a typical frame

The VRAM address only has 14 significant bits, so the unused upper two bits are used as flags to indicate horizontal or vertical sequences. If either of these is present, it indicates a multibyte sequence, and we must also specify the number of bytes we want to write.

To write a string of bytes horizontally, we combine the high byte (the upper eight bits) of the VRAM address with 0x40 using the logical-OR ("|") operator:

```
Byte 0:   [VRAM address high byte] | 0x40
Byte 1:   [VRAM address low byte]
Byte 2:   [number of bytes]
Byte 3+:  [bytes...]
```

To write a string of bytes vertically, we OR the address high byte with 0x80 instead.

0xff signals the end of packet processing for this frame:

```
Byte 0: 0xff
```

For NTSC devices, the PPU is only inactive for about 2273 cycles. This allows the NMI handler to update about 140 bytes before the PPU starts again. To be on the safe side, we cap our buffer at 128 bytes.

14.1. Using the VRAM Buffer Module

The 6502 CPU stack is assigned to the memory range $100-$1FF, but most NES games don't even use half of this area. So we put the VRAM buffer at addresses $100-$17F.

14.1 Using the VRAM Buffer Module

Open the example on 8bitworkshop.com: From the **Platforms** menu, select **Game Consoles » NES**, then select the **VRAM Buffer** project from the Project Selector dropdown.

We've bundled an easy-to-use module that manipulates the VRAM buffer. It can be included in any project like so:

```
#include "vrambuf.h"
//#link "vrambuf.c"
```

The VRAM Buffer module gives you several functions:

- **vrambuf_clear()** – Clear the VRAM buffer. Typically called at startup.
- **vrambuf_put()** – Add a packet of bytes to the VRAM buffer.
- **vrambuf_flush()** – Wait for the next video frame (allowing the NMI handler to flush the buffer to the PPU), then clear the buffer.

Our VRAM Buffer example program is similar to the example in Chapter 10, but we update the nametable each frame. Instead of writing a constant string stored in ROM, we build strings dynamically.

In our **main()** function, we need to set up the module. First we call **vrambuf_clear()** to make sure the VRAM buffer is empty. Then we call the NESLib function **set_vram_update()** to tell it where to find our VRAM buffer, and to start flushing it to the PPU before each frame.

14. VRAM Buffer

```
vrambuf_clear();
set_vram_update(updbuf);
```

In our **scroll_demo** function, we define a 32-byte local variable called str:

```
char str[32];
```

Now we initialize the string to 0 with **memset()**:

```
memset(str, 0, sizeof(str));
```

We use the built-in **sprintf()** function to build our string. This is an old-school C function that converts its parameters into human-readable characters. You have to first pass a *format string* — this one converts the first parameter into hex and the second into decimal, both padded to 6 characters:

```
sprintf(str, "%6x %6d", y, y);
```

The **vrambuf_put()** function adds a multibyte sequence to the VRAM buffer. It defaults to a horizontal sequence.

We just have to pass the VRAM address, a pointer to the byte array or string, and the number of bytes to write:

```
vrambuf_put(NTADR_A(2,y%30), str, 32);
```

A nametable has 32 columns, but only 30 rows. That's why we use the *modulo* operator (%) to keep the Y coordinate in the range 0 to 29. It essentially divides y by 30 and returns the remainder.

Note that we don't call **ppu_wait_frame()** in this loop. When the VRAM buffer is full, the **vrambuf_put()** function will call **vrambuf_flush()** to wait for the next frame before proceeding.

15

Split Status Bar

You can scroll the background in any direction on the NES. But what if you want to keep an area of the screen motionless, say for a scoreboard or status bar? This requires a *screen split*.

The NES has only one set of scroll registers. When the entire background is scrolling, they are typically set once per frame, during the NMI handler. But if you set them multiple times per frame, different regions of the screen can have different scroll values.

The CPU needs to set the scroll registers at an exact scanline to generate a stable split. How does it know when a given scanline has been reached? The most basic way is to use a *sprite zero* test.

The PPU has a *collision flag* accessible by reading the PPU_STATUS register. This flag is set whenever a background tile and the first sprite in OAM (sprite zero) collide.

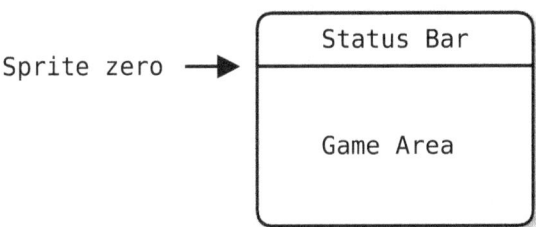

Figure 15.1: *Sprite zero placement for split screen layout.*

15. Split Status Bar

If we position sprite zero so that it's guaranteed to overlap a pixel of the background, we can poll the PPU_STATUS register and wait for it to be set. Then, we can modify the scroll registers directly in the PPU, which will take effect on the next scanline.

15.1 Setting up Sprite Zero

> Open the example on 8bitworkshop.com: From the **Platforms** menu, select **Game Consoles » NES**, then select the **Split Status Bar** project from the Project Selector dropdown.

To set up sprite zero, we use the **oam_spr()** function:

```
oam_spr(1, 30, 0xa0, 0, 0);
```

Each parameter is important, so let's go over them in order:

- **X coordinate (1):** We can position the sprite on any X coordinate from 1 to 254. X=255 doesn't work for internal reasons, and X=0 may be problematic if the PPU_MASK register has the left eight pixels masked.
- **Y coordinate (30):** NES sprites start drawing one pixel below the Y coordinate, so the sprite will appear on scanline 31. We want to start the split on scanline 32, exactly four tiles below the top of the background.
- **Tile index (0xa0):** In our pattern table, this chooses an 8-pixel wide horizontal line positioned at the top of the tile — perfect for our purposes.
- **Palette and attribute flags (0):** We don't really care which color palette the sprite uses; the collision test only cares that both background and sprite intersect on a non-transparent pixel. We could put 0x20 here if we wanted to set the priority flag and hide the pixel behind the background.
- **OAM ID (0):** This is a sprite zero test, so it's critical that this parameter is 0. Any other sprites must start at the next index (4).

15.2. Vertical Mirroring

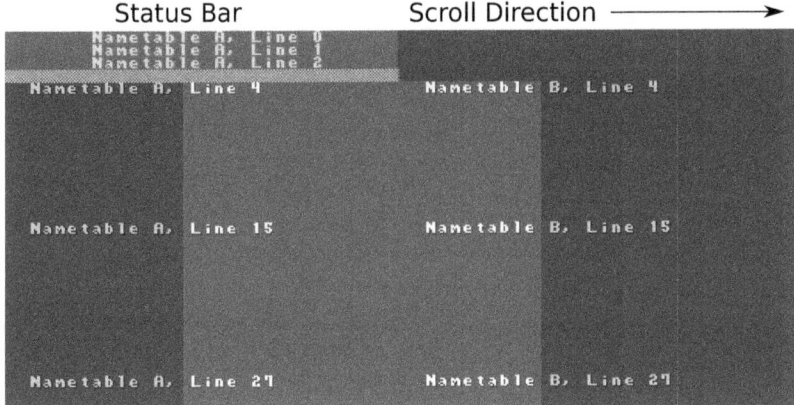

Visible Screen

15.2 Vertical Mirroring

We want to scroll the background side-to-side, below the status bar. Our previous example used the default *horizontal mirroring* method, which places the nametables above and below each other. To enable horizontal scrolling, we need to switch to *vertical mirroring*. This places the nametables beside each other.

In the **8bitworkshop IDE**, this is done with a special *preprocessor define*:

```
#define NES_MIRRORING 1     // 1 = vertical mirroring
```

This in turn changes the mirroring settings in the final ROM file's *iNES header*. Outside the IDE, you'd set this via a command-line option passed to the linker. We'll discuss this more in Chapter 34.

15.3 Calling split()

In our main loop, we must call **split()** every frame, or the split will disappear. We don't need to call **ppu_wait_nmi()**, since **split()** essentially does the same thing while waiting for the sprite zero flag.

15. Split Status Bar

ppu_wait_frame() should not be used — whenever it skips a frame, it won't perform the split and the screen will flicker. You should avoid **ppu_wait_frame()** whenever modifying PPU registers during a frame.

Our main loop will just scroll the screen from side-to-side bouncing between the two directions. It's similar to the loop in Chapter 10, except it has the **split()** function call:

```
// set scroll register
// waits for NMI, which means no frame-skip
split(x, 0);
```

split() takes two parameters, X scroll value and Y scroll value, but it ignores the Y parameter (we'll discuss this later, in Chapter 40). It keeps the CPU busy until it detects the sprite zero collision flag, then sets the X scroll register.

A few additional tips:

- Make sure there's a guaranteed pixel in the background that touches sprite zero, or **split()** may loop forever!
- Both background and sprite rendering must be enabled.
- There can be only one sprite zero hit per frame. We'll use *IRQ*s to do multiple splits in Chapter 31.
- Since the CPU wastes cycles waiting for the sprite zero flag, it's often best to place the split near the top of the screen.

▸ Play around with the parameters to **oam_spr()** that set up sprite zero. Can you move the split position up and down?

16

Random Numbers

Most games need to generate random numbers: maybe the game needs an enemy that behaves unpredictably, or requires a game element to appear at random positions on the screen. This is usually accomplished by using a *pseudorandom number generator* (PRNG). This is an algorithm that starts from a number called a *seed* and modifies it in a complex way to generate successive random numbers.

If designed correctly, the PRNG will cycle through a large range of values that do not repeat themselves, or only repeat after many thousands of iterations. This is called the PRNG's *period*.

16.1 The rand() function

NESLib provides its own PRNG, accessed via **rand8()** and **rand16()**. It's fast, but the output is not very random — it uses an 8-bit *LFSR (linear-feedback shift register)* that repeats after 255 iterations.

The **cc65** *standard library* has a function called **rand()**, which uses a 32-bit state. Although the function is slower, it takes much longer to repeat the same numbers.

16. Random Numbers

To generate random numbers between a lower and upper bound, we'll create another function called **rndint()**, which uses the *modulo* operator (%) to force the 32-bit result of **rand()** into a specific range:

```
// return a random byte between (a ... b-1)
byte rndint(byte a, byte b) {
  return (rand() % (b-a)) + a;
}
```

The *modulo* operator is fairly inefficient — this function takes about five scanlines to complete. It's more efficient to use the AND operator (&) to mask bits. For example, this expression will give you a number between zero and 15:

```
(rand() & 0xf)        // returns 0..15
```

This trick works with any power of two minus one: 1, 3, 7, 15, 31, and so on.

16.2 Entropy

If you find your random numbers are too predictable, you could add *entropy* to your PRNG. This is a source of uncertainty using random data that the algorithm pulls from unrelated sources (hardware input, for example) that makes your random number stream a little more unpredictable.

While this might make your RNG more unpredictable, it won't necessarily make it non-repeatable! If the addition of entropy makes the LFSR return to a previous value, it'll emit the same sequence again. But we're playing games, not generating cryptographic keys — experimentation will likely tell you what works and what doesn't.

An easy way to generate entropy in a game is to just call the **rand()** function every frame during the title screen. The uncertainty in when the player presses the Start button generates entropy.

17

Reading VRAM

The NES has 2 KB of RAM that the CPU can access directly, and another 2 KB of video RAM accessed via the PPU registers. We've been writing to it via **vram_write()** and other functions, but we can read from it as well. Unlike CPU RAM, you have to follow certain rules when reading.

> Open the example on 8bitworkshop.com: From the **Platforms** menu, select **Game Consoles** » **NES**, then select the **Siege Game** project from the Project Selector dropdown.

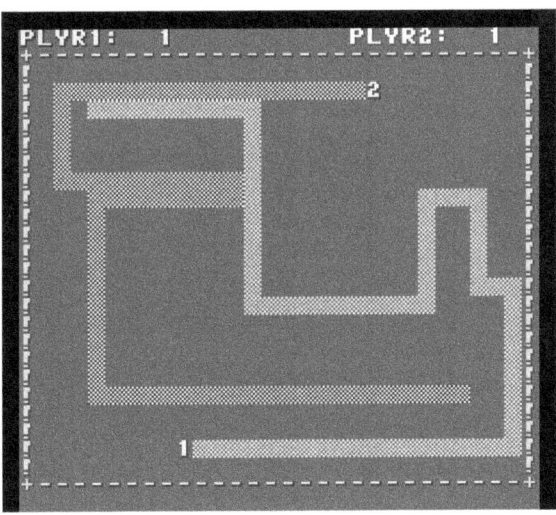

17. Reading VRAM

To demonstrate how to read video RAM, we'll look at the *Siege Game* example, which is described in my earlier book, *Making 8-bit Arcade Games in C*. It features two players who leave walls behind them as they travel around the playfield. These walls are written to the nametable, where they are also displayed on the screen.

To see if a player collides with a wall fragment, the CPU needs to read back this data. We could mirror the wall data in CPU RAM, but reading it directly from video RAM is a more efficient use of memory.

Reading from *video RAM* is similar to writing to it:

1. Make sure the PPU is turned off or in *vertical blank* (i.e., not rendering).
2. Set the address to read in `PPU_ADDR`.
3. Read the data from `PPU_DATA`.
4. The address will *auto-increment*, so keep reading `PPU_DATA` until the desired number of bytes are read.
5. Before rendering starts, set the address of the upper-left of the nametable in `PPU_ADDR`. This prevents corruption of the video frame.

Let's write this up in C. First, we compute the VRAM address to read, from X and Y coordinates:

```
byte getchar(byte x, byte y) {
  word addr = NTADR_A(x,y);
  byte rd;             // result will go here
```

> Note that we start this function definition with `byte` instead of `void`. This gives the function a *return type* of `byte`, an 8-bit unsigned value. The **return** keyword sends a value of type `byte` back to the caller.

Now we wait for *vertical blank* to start, when the PPU becomes inactive. We can use **ppu_wait_nmi()** here, since we really don't want to waste time skipping a frame.

```
ppu_wait_nmi();         // wait for vblank
```

Now we use **vram_adr()** to set the PPU address, and **vram_read()** to read a single byte into the rd variable:

```
vram_adr(addr);         // set address
vram_read(&rd, 1);      // read 1 byte into rd
```

The & symbol (when placed before an expression, as it is here) is the *address-of operator*. This passes the memory location of the rd variable to the **vram_read()** function, which allows it to store data back into the variable.

Setting the VRAM address has an unfortunate side effect: It corrupts the internal scroll registers which determine the starting position of the video frame. To prevent a "jumping" effect, we have to reset these registers. This is normally done by the *NMI handler* in *NESLib*, but our code runs after the NMI handler has already returned.

We'll have to reset the registers ourselves. Since this game doesn't use scrolling, and only uses the first nametable, we can just set the PPU address to 0:

```
vram_adr(0x0);          // fix scroll
```

When we were using the *VRAM buffer* functions in Chapter 14, the VRAM updates took place inside of the NMI handler, which set the scroll registers before returning. Basically, if we call **vram_adr()** anytime when the PPU is active, we're going to have this problem. The one exception is using **split()** which also sets the registers correctly before returning.

The last thing we do in the **getchar()** function is return the rd variable, which contains the value read by **vram_read()**:

```
return rd;              // return result
```

You can read from any address accessed by the PPU, including the pattern tables. One very popular NES game stores the

17. Reading VRAM

data for its title screen in CHR ROM — the CPU copies it into nametable RAM at startup.

You can also store metadata about a level in the nametable, then read it back during the game. The example *Shiru's Chase Game* stores spawn points this way.

> ▶ Think about the previous chapter with the scrolling randomly-generated buildings. How would you detect collisions between actors and the buildings? If it's not practical to read from video RAM, could you store a list of building heights in CPU RAM?

18

PPU Mask Register

The PPU lets you selectively enable the background or sprite layer for output. If you omit both of these, the display is turned off. NESLib has several handy functions for setting these:

```
ppu_on_all();   // turn on background + sprites
ppu_on_bg();    // turn on background only
ppu_on_spr();   // turn on sprites only
ppu_off();      // turn off rendering
```

These functions do no more than set a *shadow register* which updates the PPU_MASK register during the next NMI. You can set the shadow directly with *ppu_mask()*. For example, **ppu_on_all()** is the same as this:

```
ppu_mask(MASK_BG|MASK_SPR);
```

By default, the leftmost eight pixels in the background and sprite layers are hidden. This is used to hide offscreen updates when scrolling to the left. You can un-hide them by setting the MASK_EDGE flags:

```
ppu_mask(MASK_BG|MASK_SPR|MASK_EDGE_BG|MASK_EDGE_SPR);
```

Note that we also set the MASK_BG and MASK_SPR flags to keep the PPU display turned on.

18. PPU Mask Register

 Open the example on 8bitworkshop.com: From the **Platforms** menu, select **Game Consoles » NES**, then select the **Color Emphasis** project from the Project Selector dropdown.

There are three *color emphasis* flags that accentuate the red, green, or blue tint of the entire screen. For example, to emphasize blue:

```
ppu_mask(MASK_BG|MASK_SPR|MASK_TINT_BLUE);
```

Setting all three tint flags is an easy way to dim the screen:

```
ppu_mask(MASK_BG|MASK_SPR
    |MASK_TINT_BLUE|MASK_TINT_GREEN|MASK_TINT_RED);
```

There's also a `MASK_MONO` flag that turns the entire screen to grayscale:

```
ppu_mask(MASK_BG|MASK_SPR|MASK_MONO);
```

If tint flags are present, they are applied after the grayscale effect.

You can also read and write the `PPU_CTRL` shadow register directly, if needed:

```
set_ppu_ctrl_var(get_ppu_ctrl_var() | 0x20);
```

However, NESLib manages `PPU_CTRL` through several functions, so this is not often necessary.

19

Virtual Bright

NESLib supports a feature called *virtual bright* that makes it easy to perform *palette fades*. You know how some games fade in or out from a completely black or white screen? This is what we're talking about.

> ▶ Open the example on 8bitworkshop.com: From the **Platforms** menu, select **Game Consoles** » **NES**, then select the **Title Screen RLE** project from the Project Selector dropdown.

Whenever you use one of the pal_xxx functions to change palette colors, you're actually modifying an internal palette in RAM,

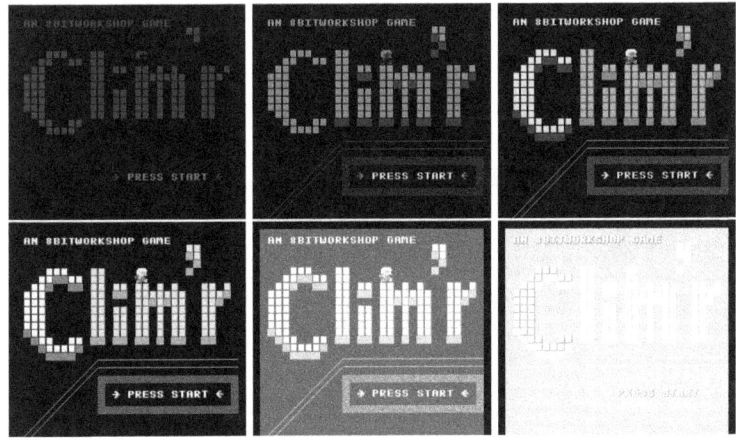

19. Virtual Bright

not the PPU hardware directly. The *NMI handler* detects if the internal palette has changed, and if so, sends the changes to the PPU. Before it does, it modifies the palette according to the virtual bright lookup table.

The virtual bright lookup table is laid out with 64 bytes of total black, 64 bytes of the standard NES colors, and 64 bytes of total white:

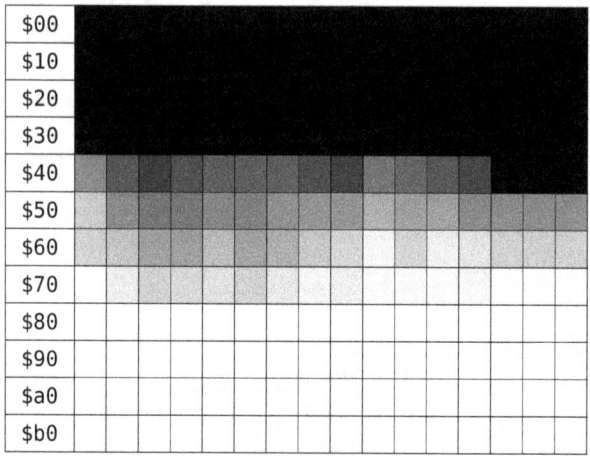

Note how the colors get brighter on each successive row. When choosing palette colors, NESLib looks at four consecutive rows of this table. By simply sliding around the four-row window from offset $00 to offset $80, nine levels of brightness from total black to total white are possible.

The **pal_bright()** function sets the virtual bright level. Zero is total black, eight is total white, and four is normal colors. Everything in between is darker or brighter than normal.

For example, you could fade-in from black by calling **pal_bright()** with values from 0 to 4, using **ppu_wait_frame()** to delay a few frames between calls.

 What other kinds of screen effects do you think you could achieve using virtual bright?

20

The APU

The *Audio Processing Unit* (*APU*) is a sound generator packaged with the CPU in the RP2A03 chip. It has five independent sound generators, or *channels*.

The pulse and triangle channels output clear tones, useful for music or sound effects. The noise channel is good for drums, explosions, and the like. The DMC channel is special; it reads from *PRG ROM* to play 7-bit sampled audio, though it's not often used.

A channel may have an *envelope* which makes the sound decay at a configurable rate. It may also have a *length counter* which makes the sound end after a configurable duration. These are both driven by the *frame counter*, a 240 Hz clock.

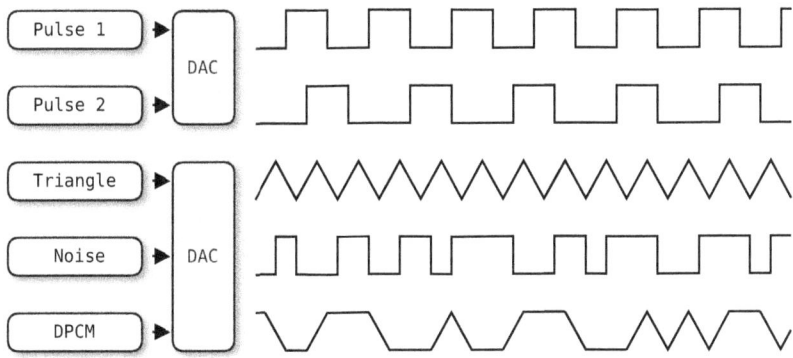

Figure 20.1: APU Sound Generators

20. THE APU

Each channel has a configurable *frequency* controlled by a 11-bit divisor or 4-bit lookup table. For the pulse and triangle channels, the output frequency is given by this equation:

$F = 1789773/(16*(D+1))$

The pulse channels have a couple of extra features. They have a configurable *duty cycle* which can make a note sound thin and reedy at lower values, or full-bodied at higher values. They also have a *sweep* feature which makes the pitch of the note rise or fall continuously.

Type	Output	Freq. Bits	Envelope?	Sweep?
Pulse 1	Square wave	11	X	X
Pulse 2	Square wave	11	X	X
Triangle	Triangle wave	11		
Noise	Pseudorandom	4	X	
DMC	7-bit samples	4		

> Open the example on 8bitworkshop.com: From the **Platforms** menu, select **Game Consoles » NES**, then select the **Sound Tester** project from the Project Selector dropdown.

Figure 20.2: Sound Tester Demo

We've included a helpful library with macros for setting APU registers. You can include it using the following directives:

```
#include "apu.h"
//#link "apu.c"
```

You should run the initialization routine, **apu_init()**, on program startup. It sets all the APU's registers to initial values.

There are also several *macro*s to allow easy setting of APU registers. First, the APU_ENABLE macro allows you to enable any combination of channels, given by a bitmask:

```
APU_ENABLE(flags)

flags = ENABLE_PULSE0 | ENABLE_PULSE1 | ENABLE_TRIANGLE
      | ENABLE_NOISE | ENABLE_DMC
```

There are macros to set pulse and triangle channel parameters. The pulse channels have multiple variants depending on whether you want a note to decay, sustain, or control an existing note.

```
APU_PULSE_DECAY(channel,period,duty,decay,len)
APU_PULSE_SET_DECAY(channel,duty,decay)
APU_PULSE_SET_VOLUME(channel,duty,vol)
APU_TRIANGLE_LENGTH(period,len)
APU_TRIANGLE_SUSTAIN(period)

channel = PULSE_CH0 | PULSE_CH1
period  = divisor from 0 to 2047 (0x7ff)
duty    = DUTY_12 | DUTY_25 | DUTY_50 | DUTY_75
decay   = 0 (fast) to 15 (slow)
len     = duration in frames from 0 to 31
```

You can also control the pulse generators' sweep units via macros:

```
APU_PULSE_SWEEP(channel,period,shift,up)
APU_PULSE_SWEEP_DISABLE(channel)

channel = PULSE_CH0 | PULSE_CH1
period  = sweep period from 0 (smooth) to 7 (glitchy)
shift   = sweep rate from 0 (fast) to 7 (slow)
up      = sweep up (1) or down (0)
```

20. The APU

The noise channel has similar macros:

```
APU_NOISE_SUSTAIN(_period,vol)
APU_NOISE_DECAY(_period,_decay,_len)

_period = rate from 0 to 15
vol     = volume from 0 to 15
```

20.1 Length Counter

Each channel has an optional *length counter* — this is independent from the decay rate. A channel must first be enabled before its length counter value is set. After the value is set, it counts down at the rate of 120 times a second. When it hits zero, the channel is silenced.

When you set a length counter, the actual value is determined by a lookup table, given in Figure 20.3. One half (odd values) maps to a linear scale. The other half (even values) is for music – there are eight different note durations at two different tempos.

The APU.status register returns the enable state of each length counter. A music player could use this to determine when to play new notes.

Linear Values (odd)				Normal Music		Faster Music		Ratio
$1F	30	$0F	14	$1E	32	$0E	26	1/6
$1D	28	$0D	12	$1C	16	$0C	14	1/12
$1B	26	$0B	10	$1A	72	$0A	60	3/8
$19	24	$09	8	$18	192	$08	160	1
$17	22	$07	6	$16	96	$06	80	1/2
$15	20	$05	4	$14	48	$04	40	1/4
$13	18	$03	2	$12	24	$02	20	1/8
$11	16	$01	254	$10	12	$00	10	1/16

Figure 20.3: APU Lookup Table

20.2 Examples

In the *Solarian* example game, we use these macros to generate sound effects.

For example, for the player's missile firing, we modify the frequency based on the Y position of the missile.

20.2. Examples

```
if (missiles[PLYRMISSILE].ypos != YOFFSCREEN) {
  APU_PULSE_SUSTAIN(0, 255-missiles[PLYRMISSILE].ypos,
    DUTY_50, 6);
} else {
  APU_PULSE_SET_VOLUME(0, DUTY_50, 0);
}
```

We use the noise channel for explosions:

```
if (player_exploding && player_exploding < 8) {
  APU_NOISE_DECAY(8 + player_exploding, 5, 15);
} else if (enemy_exploding) {
  APU_NOISE_DECAY(8 + enemy_exploding, 2, 8);
}
```

We use the triangle channel for the diving sounds of the attackers, looking for the first attacker and using their Y coordinate:

```
APU_TRIANGLE_SUSTAIN(0x100 | y);
enable |= ENABLE_TRIANGLE;
```

Note that we use the `|=` operator, which does a bitwise-OR between a variable and another value, then stores the result back into the variable.

We keep track of all of the channels enabled in the `enable` variable. This is especially important with the triangle channel, since its volume cannot be controlled nor can it decay:

```
APU_ENABLE(enable);
```

Yes, since we are using the length counter, we should enable channels first, not last! This would be an issue if we were just writing to the APU once, but since we're updating it 50 or 60 times a second, it won't be noticeable.

▶ Go to the *Siege Game* example and see if you can add sound effects using the apu functions. You'll have to first add the #include and #link directives listed above.

21

Simple Music

Playing music on the NES *APU* is just a matter of setting the right frequencies at the right times (isn't that true of all music?).

 Open the example on 8bitworkshop.com: From the **Platforms** menu, select **Game Consoles » NES**, then select the **Music Player** project from the Project Selector dropdown.

21.1 Hitting the Right Note

First, we need to create a table that maps musical notes to their period register values. If we count the first key on a standard 88-key piano as 1, the frequency of a note is given by this equation:

$$F_{A4} \cdot \frac{2^{(note-49)}}{12}$$

F_{A4} is the frequency of the musical note A above middle C, often called A4 or A440, since its standard frequency is 440 Hz.

Since the APU registers can only store integer values, we cannot get all notes exactly on pitch. The tuning error increases rapidly as the notes get higher in pitch, since the integer divisor gets closer to zero.

However, we can choose a value for A4 to minimize the tuning error in a certain note range. Generally, we have to give up accuracy in higher frequencies to get more accurate lower frequencies.

We've provided a Python script (**mknotes.py**)[1] that figures out the best A4 value for a given range of notes, and then generates a C array containing the Tone Period register values for all of the notes. Its first parameter is the highest note to optimize, and the second parameter is the number of notes to output. For example:

```
python3 mknotes.py -f 111860.8 -l 64 -u 49
```

In the code, we've included a few different frequency tables. You can change this macro to hear the subtle differences between them:

```
#define NOTE_TABLE note_table_49
```

21.2 Laying out the Score

Now we just need to list the notes we want to play in order, right?

```
const byte music_score_all_at_once[] = {
  0x2c,0x0d,0x2e,0x2f,0x2e,0x0d,0x2c,0x12 ...
};
```

Not so fast! We also need to know how much time elapses between each note, or each set of notes.

If the high bit is set, we decode the byte as a duration. When we hit a duration byte, we pause for the given number of video frames ($duration$/60 sec), which sustains the notes.

---

[1]https://8bitworkshop.com/release/8bitworkshop-tools.zip

```
const byte music_score[] = {
        0x2c, // note 44
        0x81, // duration 1
        0x0d, // note 13
        0x8d, // duration 13
        0x2e, // note 46
        0x2f, // note 47
        0x86, // duration 6
        ...
};
```

We only have three non-noise channels in the APU (two pulse + one triangle), so we can only play three notes at a time. If we try to play a fourth note while three are playing, we'll have to either ignore it or interrupt another note.

21.3 Swinging with the Tempo

Every video frame, we'll call **play_music()** to update the APU values.

The next step is to play new notes. If cur_duration is zero, we fetch the next byte from the music data:

```
// run out duration timer yet?
while (cur_duration == 0) {
  // fetch next byte in score
  byte note = next_music_byte();
```

If the byte's high bit is not set, it's not a note. It's a duration:

```
// set duration until next note
cur_duration = note & 63;
```

Otherwise, it's a note value. We've got three channels (two pulse, one triangle) to work with, but we treat them differently. We try to assign lower notes to the triangle channel, and the rest to the pulse channels.

We also keep a bitmask variable (ch) that tracks which channels are active and resets to zero whenever a duration value is read. This lets us assign notes to unused channels.

There's a different code branch to handle each channel:

```
// if this a high note, or the triangle
// channel is occupied, use pulse channels
if (note >= BASS_NOTE || (chs & 4)) {
  int period = NOTE_TABLE[note & 63];
  // see which pulse generator is free
  if (!(chs & 1)) {
    APU_PULSE_DECAY(0, period, DUTY_25, 2, 10);
    chs |= 1;
  } else if (!(chs & 2)) {
    APU_PULSE_DECAY(1, period, DUTY_25, 2, 10);
    chs |= 2;
  }
} else {
  int period = note_table_tri[note & 63];
  APU_TRIANGLE_LENGTH(period, 15);
  chs |= 4;
}
```

The APU handles the volume envelope via the decay and duration parameters. We don't have to touch the sound channel registers again until a new note comes along.

21.4 Composing the Music

But where does the music data come from? We've created a Python script, **midi2song.py** (also located in the 8bitworkshop Tools file) that converts a MIDI file into a music data array. First, install the dependency mido and then pass the script a filename to view the MIDI file:

```
$ pip3 install mido
$ python3 midi2song.py morning.mid
```

```
<midi file 'morning.mid' type 1, 13 tracks, 2612 messages>
184.050417521 seconds
Track 0:  (105) []
Track 1: Words (165) []
Track 2: Guitar (1642) [1]
Track 3: Flute (325) [2]
Track 4: Piano (317) [3]
```

You might see just one track, or several tracks. The numbers in [brackets] are the MIDI channels used by each track; sometimes

21.4. Composing the Music

all of the channels are jammed into a single track. To convert a file, pass a comma-separated list of the channels (not the track numbers!) you wish to translate. For this example, we probably want to use channels 1, 2, and 3:

```
$ python midi2song.py morning.mid 1,2,3
```

The script will then parse the MIDI file and output a C array that you can copy and paste into your C source file.

You can also pass a third parameter which transposes the MIDI notes by the desired number of half-steps (negative = down, positive = up).

The Mutopia Project (mutopiaproject.org) has public domain MIDI files converted from musical scores. The Scott Joplin rags work pretty well for game music.

In Chapter 22, we'll discuss the *FamiTone2* tracker and library, which unifies music and sound effects and allows for much more complex compositions.

22

FamiTone Music

While we learned how to play simple music on the NES in Chapter 21, many homebrew games implement more complex music using a *tracker* and associated playback library.

A *tracker* is a tool that lets you compose complex musical tracks, featuring multiple instruments and effects. Instead of converting from a MIDI file, the tracker lets you closely control the hardware of the target system, and saves the musical track in a special format.

At runtime, a library parses this format and can play it back on command.

The most popular tracker for NES is **FamiTracker** for Windows, which you can use to export source code that you can link to your project like any other file. FamiTracker can be downloaded from http://www.famitracker.com/downloads.php.

If you don't have access to a Windows machine, Famitracker runs well under the **Wine** emulator.

FamiTracker's associated playback library is **FamiTone2**, which we can reference in our C code. It not only plays music, but can mix multiple streams to add sound effects.

22. FamiTone Music

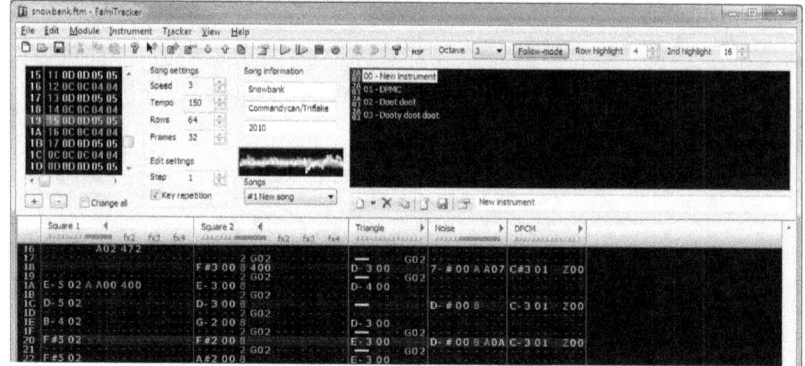

Figure 22.1: FamiTracker screenshot

22.1 FamiTone in C

> Open the example on 8bitworkshop.com: From the
> **Platforms** menu, select **Game Consoles** » **NES**, then
> select the **FamiTone Demo** project from the Project
> Selector dropdown.

Using the FamiTone2 library in C is fairly straightforward. First we link the library, contained in an assembly file:

```
//#link "famitone2.s"
```

Next, we declare the prototype for the **famitone_update()** function, which should run every video frame. We'll later connect it to the NMI handler:

```
void __fastcall__ famitone_update(void);
```

We also need some tracks to play. We'll include two music files and one sound effect file:

```
//#link "music_aftertherain.s"
extern char after_the_rain_music_data[];
//#link "music_dangerstreets.s"
extern char danger_streets_music_data[];
//#link "demosounds.s"
extern char demo_sounds[];
```

22.1. FamiTone in C

These can be exported from **FamiTracker**. Some massaging may be necessary to get them into the **ca65** assembly format.

Now we initialize the FamiTone library. We pass the music and sound effect data separately — they can each contain multiple tracks:

```
famitone_init(danger_streets_music_data);
sfx_init(demo_sounds);
```

We now connect the NMI handler to our FamiTone update function.

```
nmi_set_callback(famitone_update);
```

Note that we could also define our own NMI handler function, then call **famitone_update()** from it.

This is how you start music playback:

```
music_play(0);
```

This is how you play a sound effect — the first parameter is the sound effect number, the second is the sound effect stream:

```
sfx_play(0,1);   // play effect 0 on channel 1
```

FamiTone can be configured with zero to four sound effect streams. Each stream is evaluated, but a louder sound will take priority over quieter sound or music. For example, an explosion and a snare drum may both use the noise channel, but whichever is louder at the moment will be programmed into the APU.

> ▸ Go to the *Siege Game* example and try adding music and sound effects using the FamiTone library. You'll have to copy-and-paste the #link and extern directives and the **famitone_update()** function declaration from the example file. You'll also have to initialize with **famitone_init()** and **sfx_init()** as described above.

23

Binary-Coded Decimals

Up to this point, we've only dealt with bytes encoded in binary — which represent unsigned values from 0 to 255. Now we're going to use *binary-coded decimal* or *BCD* values.

BCD represents numbers in a more human-readable format. Bytes are split in half, into two 4-bit *nibbles*, each containing a decimal digit from 0 to 9.

In this scheme, the hexadecimal value reads the same as the decimal representation. For example, $00 to $09 are the same, but 10 is stored as $10, 11 is $11 12 is $12, etc. all the way up to $99.

You can represent more digits by just tacking on more bytes. For example, a two-byte value can represent a four-digit number. Here's "3905" encoded in BCD:

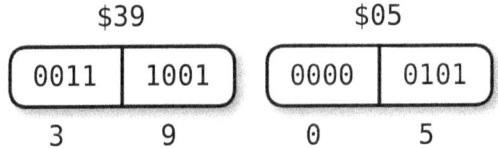

Some early computers used the BCD representation for their number-crunching, and mainframes used them for processing financial data. They are still handy in the 8-bit world, foremost because they are easier to render to the screen. We don't have

23. Binary-Coded Decimals

to divide by 10 to convert them to decimal digits, because the decimal digits are already part of the representation.

To extract the two digits from a BCD byte, we just shift by 4 to isolate the first digit (the high nibble) and mask by binary %1111 ($0F) to isolate the second digit (the low nibble):

```
void bcd2digits(byte bcd) {
  char digit1 = '0' + (bcd >> 4);
  char digit2 = '0' + (bcd & 0xf);
  ...
}
```

In C, we might find it handy to operate with 16-bit BCD numbers, which hold a total of 4 decimal digits. Here's a function to render all 4 digits to a given X/Y position on the screen, by shifting and masking each successive digit:

```
void draw_bcd_word(byte x, byte y, word bcd) {
  byte j;
  x += 3;
  for (j=0; j<4; j++) {
    putchar(x, y, CHAR('0'+(bcd & 0xf)));
    x--;
    bcd >>= 4;
  }
}
```

23.1 BCD Addition

We might want to add two 16-bit BCD numbers, for instance to add to a player's score. The 6502 can do BCD arithmetic by setting its Decimal flag. In the NES, this functionality was omitted to free up silicon real estate. However, we can implement our own BCD routines.

We could do this the same way you might do it on paper, by adding over each pair of digits and carrying the ones. This is pretty simple, but it requires we loop four times and perform a lot of bit-shifts, which are expensive on the 6502.

It'd be nice if we could use the built-in ADC (add with carry) instruction, because binary addition is correct with BCD if no

23.1. BCD Addition

digits carry over. For example, $1234 + $1234 = $2468. We have to then fix the digits that carried, which is a bit of trickery:

```
word bcd_add(word a, word b) {
  register word c, d;        // intermediate values
  c = a + 0x0666;            // add 6 to each BCD digit
  d = c ^ b;                 // sum without carry propagation
  c += b;                    // provisional sum
  d = ~(c ^ d) & 0x1110;     // just the BCD carry bits
  d = (d >> 2) | (d >> 3);   // correction
  return c - d;              // corrected BCD sum
}
```

The trick is to add the BCD numbers, then add 6 to each BCD digit except the last. This forces a carry in each BCD digit, since any digits that added to 10 or above will wrap around to 16 or higher. For example, $1234 + $5678 + $666 = $6F12.

Note that each digit that carried over is correct, but the third digit is $F. In the next step, we detect and isolate the carry bits. The final step subtracts 6 from each BCD digit that carried over. (Hey, some smart people came up with this and it works, okay?)

This function is in the file **bcd.c**. You can access it via the #include and //#link directives:

```
#include "bcd.h"
//#link "bcd.c"
```

Example usage:

```
word score = 0x0;               // 4-digit (16-bit) BCD
score = bcd_add(score, 0x25);   // add 25 to score
```

This function takes about five scanlines to complete, so avoid using it in loops.

24

RLE Encoding and Title Screens

RLE (or *run-length encoding*) is a simple data compression method. It is especially popular on constrained systems like the 6502, and on the NES, it's useful for compressing *tilemaps*.

RLE takes advantage of duplicated bytes in data streams. It collapses these "runs" of identical bytes into a smaller encoding, which is expanded to the original stream of bytes when decompressed.

Figure 24.1: Title screen unpacked from RLE-compressed data

24. RLE Encoding and Title Screens

There are many competing RLE formats. The variant of RLE used in NESLib uses a *tag byte* to distinguish runs from uncompressed data. The tag byte appears in the compressed stream followed by a *count byte*. The decompressor replaces these two bytes by N copies of the most recent data byte, where N is the count byte. Here's some sample RLE-compressed data:

```
01              initial byte defines tag byte = 0x01
00              data (0x00)
01 a3           run  (0xa3 copies of 0x00)
10              data (0x10)
01 04           run  (0x04 copies of 0x10)
00 10           data (0x00 0x10)
...
```

Luckily, we don't have to write RLE data by hand. Handy tools are available for compressing and decompressing RLE data on the NES. We'll use one such tool below.

24.1 Compressing Nametables

Nametables are one of the most common uses of RLE-compressed data. They compress well, since they often contain large regions of repeated data.

> Open the example on 8bitworkshop.com: From the
> **Platforms** menu, select **Game Consoles » NES**, then
> select the **Title Screen RLE** project from the Project
> Selector dropdown.

We used Shiru's **NES Screen Tool** to draw this title screen (**NES Screen Tool** can be downloaded from https://shiru.untergrund.net/software.shtml). We then saved the palette to a .pal file and downloaded the RLE packed binary .rle files (**Nametable » Save Nametable and Attributes**).

We then used a command-line tool called **hexdump** to convert them to .byte statements to be included in an assembly .s file:

```
cat <filename> | hexdump -v -e '" \n .byte  " 32/1 "$$%02x,"'
    | cut -c 2-135
```

24.1. Compressing Nametables

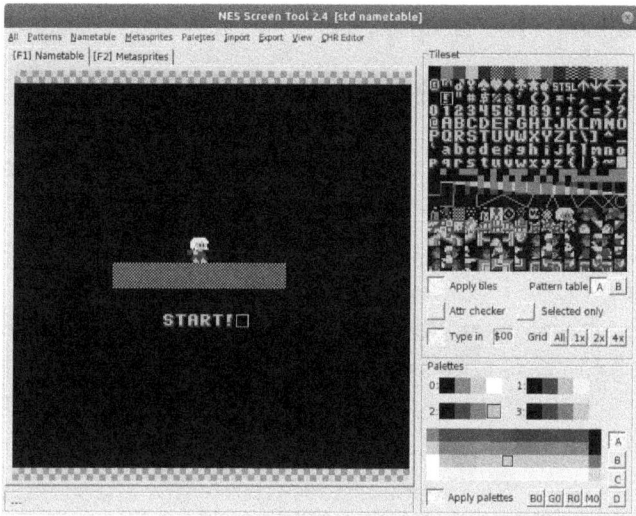

Figure 24.2: NES Screen Tool.

We make the data available to C programs like this:

```
.export _climbr_title_rle
_climbr_title_rle:
 .byte $01,$00,$01,$10,$80,$01,$02,$00
 .byte ...
```

We can then import the data in our C program using the **extern** keyword:

```
extern const byte climbr_title_rle[];
```

To unpack the nametable, we must first set the PPU address with **vram_adr()**. Then we call **vram_unrle()**, passing a pointer to the RLE-compressed data:

```
// unpack nametable into the VRAM
vram_adr(0x2000);
vram_unrle(climbr_title_rle);
```

This is not a fast operation — it takes about 160 scanlines to unpack an entire nametable and it can only be done while the PPU is turned off.

117

24.2 Other Techniques

You can also use compression for the pattern table. RLE isn't always the best method, since bitmaps often contain more varied data than nametables. Sometimes, custom compression methods are used.

Modern games might use a *sliding-window compression* method such as *LZ4*. For example, the default CHR file we use in this book compresses by 25% using LZ4. NESLib can decompress this format with **vram_unlz4()**, but it is several times slower than decompressing RLE, due to the difficulty of reading from video RAM.

There are other RLE formats that work while the game is running, updating during the vertical blank period. The concept is similar to the *VRAM buffer* system described in Chapter 14.

Compressed level data is stored in ROM, but in a format that makes it easy to extract one *stripe* at a time. For example, a horizontally scrolling game might have vertical sections 2 to 16 tiles wide. Some of these systems operate on 2x2 or 4x4 blocks called *metatiles*, making attribute table manipulation simpler.

25

Offscreen Scrolling

The NES has enough RAM for two nametables — two complete screens of background data. How do games scroll through a world that spans dozens of different screens?

The solution is to draw *offscreen*, updating the portion of the nametable that is not yet visible. If we do this correctly, the player will never see what we're doing offscreen as we scroll through the world.

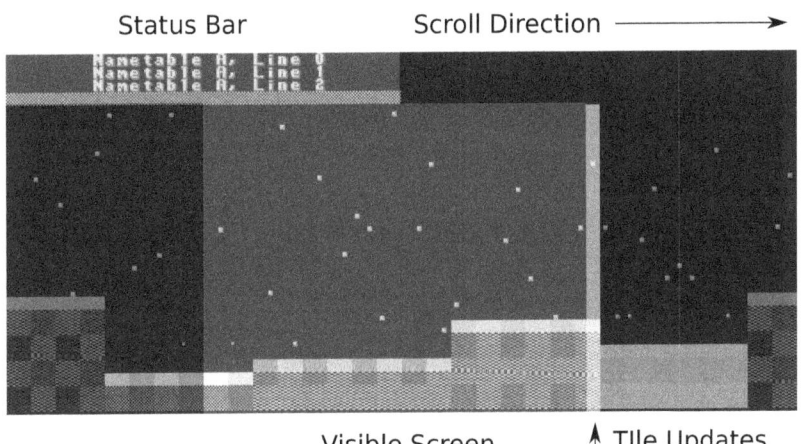

25. Offscreen Scrolling

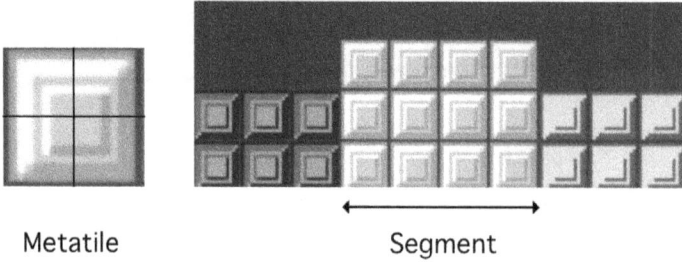

Metatile   Segment

> Open the example on 8bitworkshop.com: From the **Platforms** menu, select **Game Consoles** » **NES**, then select the **Offscreen Scrolling** project from the Project Selector dropdown.

The Offscreen Scrolling demo generates an endless random game level, scrolling continuously to the left. The level is composed of *metatiles*. Each metatile is a 2x2 block of tiles (16 pixels square).

Every 16 pixels, we'll write a stack of metatiles — that is, we'll write two 8-pixel-wide columns to the nametable. When this 16-pixel-wide stack scrolls completely into view, we'll draw the next stack, and so forth.

Our randomly-generated level will be divided into *segment*s. Each segment is a variable number of metatiles wide, and has a common set of attributes. This demo has very simple segments, with only variable width, height, and color.

We'll use the *VRAM buffer* module from Chapter 14 to update the nametable while the PPU is active. Some of the setup code is similar to the "Split Status Bar" example from Chapter 15.

We need a variable to track the horizontal scroll position:

```
word x_scroll;          // X scroll amount in pixels
```

For this demo, we only need to keep track of the segment currently being drawn offscreen. These global variables hold the segment data.

```
byte seg_height;        // segment height in metatiles
byte seg_width;         // segment width in metatiles
byte seg_char;          // character to draw
byte seg_palette;       // attribute table value
```

Whenever we need a new segment, we'll fill these values randomly by calling the **new_segment()** function. It uses NESLib's **rand8()** function, which returns a random value between 0 and 255. We use a bitmask to reduce their range:

```
void new_segment() {
  seg_height = (rand8() & 3) + 1;  // 1..4
  seg_width = (rand8() & 3) + 1;   // 1..4
  seg_palette = rand8() & 3;       // 0..3
  seg_char = 0xf4;                 // tile index
}
```

This gives us a random segment height and width (in metatiles), character tile index, and palette index. We'll use these attributes to draw offscreen tiles until the next segment comes along.

25.1 Drawing Metatiles

Our active play area is only 24 tiles high because we have a split status bar. We put this value in a constant named PLAYROWS:

```
#define PLAYROWS 24
```

Since a metatile is two tiles wide, we'll draw two columns at a time. We'll define a byte array for each column:

```
char ntbuf1[PLAYROWS];  // left side column
char ntbuf2[PLAYROWS];  // right side column
```

We'll store nametable data here until we're ready to write them into the VRAM buffer. The function **set_metatile()** draws a metatile into these arrays at a given Y position:

```
void set_metatile(byte y, byte ch) {
  ntbuf1[y*2] = ch;        // upper-left
  ntbuf1[y*2+1] = ch+1;    // lower-left
  ntbuf2[y*2] = ch+2;      // upper-right
  ntbuf2[y*2+1] = ch+3;    // lower-right
}
```

25. Offscreen Scrolling

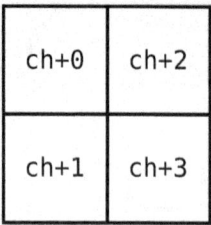

Figure 25.1: Metatile layout

The function **fill_buffer()** draws the entire stack of metatiles. First, we clear both nametable arrays:

```
void fill_buffer(byte x) {
  byte i,y;
  // clear nametable buffers
  memset(ntbuf1, 0, sizeof(ntbuf1));
  memset(ntbuf2, 0, sizeof(ntbuf2));
```

Our background will be a random starfield. To get each star's Y position, we get a random value from **rand8()** and mask it to the range 0 through 15. We then write a period character into the ntbuf1 array at that index:

```
  ntbuf1[rand8() & 15] = '.';
```

Our segment is a variable number of metatiles high. We draw the stack of metatiles, starting from the bottom, calling **set_metatile()** for each one.

```
  for (i=0; i<seg_height; i++) {
    y = PLAYROWS/2-1-i;
    set_metatile(y, seg_char);
    set_attr_entry(x, y, seg_palette);
  }
}
```

Note that we also call a function called **set_attr_entry()**. It sets the palette of each metatile in the *attribute table*. We'll explain this function in a bit.

25.2 Coloring Metatiles

We chose the 2x2 size for metatiles for a good reason. Because they're the same size, the metatile grid aligns to the attribute table grid, and thus each metatile can have a different palette (refer to Figure 9.2 if you need a refresher).

We also need an array to store attribute table bytes for the current stack being drawn offscreen. Each attribute table byte determines palettes for a 4x4 section of tiles. Thus, this array need only be ¼ the size of the nametable arrays:

```
char attrbuf[PLAYROWS/4];    // 24/4 = 6 bytes long
```

set_attr_entry() sets an entry in this array for a given palette index (0-3). We need both X and Y metatile coordinates, because we can either set the left or right side of the attribute block:

```
void set_attr_entry(byte x, byte y, byte pal) {
  if (y&1) pal <<= 4;   // entry on the bottom?
  if (x&1) pal <<= 2;   // entry on the right?
  attrbuf[y/2] |= pal;  // OR with existing byte
}
```

Note that the attribute block covers a 4x4 tile square, but we update the attribute table every 2 columns. So we actually end up setting each attribute table byte in VRAM twice. This is desirable because our offscreen column is so close to the visible edge that we see the left side of the attribute table block before we get around to setting the right side.

25.3 Drawing Metatiles to the VRAM Buffer

Now that we've set up our ntbuf and attrbuf arrays, it's time to write them to the VRAM buffer. But first we need to calculate the nametable address where we'll start writing, where the offscreen portion starts.

Our X scroll position has a valid range of 0 to 511. We'll convert the X scroll position (in pixels) to X nametable column (in tiles):

```
x = (x_scroll/8 + 32) & 63;
```

Our target is 32 tiles to the right of the leftmost tile, just off the right edge of the screen. (We could go all the way up to 60, as long as it's a multiple of four.)

Now we compute the nametable address, starting below the status bar (row 4). If the X column is between 0 and 31, we update nametable A. If between 32 and 63, we update nametable B:

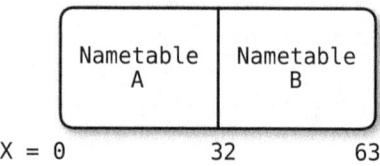

(See Figure 10.3 if you need a refresher on vertical mirroring.) We compute addr, the nametable address, like this:

```
if (x < 32)
   addr = NTADR_A(x, 4);
else
   addr = NTADR_B(x&31, 4);
```

Now we're going to write a vertical slice of tiles starting at that address. We use **vrambuf_put()** to write both nametable buffers to the VRAM buffer:

```
// draw vertical slice from ntbuf arrays to name table
// starting with leftmost slice
vrambuf_put(addr | VRAMBUF_VERT, ntbuf1, PLAYROWS);
// then the rightmost slice
vrambuf_put((addr+1) | VRAMBUF_VERT, ntbuf2, PLAYROWS);
```

We use the bitwise-OR operator (|) to combine the nametable address with the VRAMBUF_VERT flag. This tells the VRAM buffer routine to draw the buffer vertically instead of horizontally, starting at the given address.

25.4 Setting Attribute Blocks

We already know the address in the nametable — it'd be nice if we could find the corresponding attribute block address. We

25.4. Setting Attribute Blocks

can do this with a few ANDs, ORs, and shifts. We'll put this logic in the **nt2attraddr()** function:

```
word nt2attraddr(word a) {
  return (a & 0x2c00)          // mask nametable origin
       | 0x3c0                 // start of attribute table
       | ((a >> 4) & 0x38)     // row
       | ((a >> 2) & 0x07);    // column
}
```

This function looks complicated — and it is! But it's just choosing certain bits from the nametable address to form the attribute block address, essentially dividing the row and column by two. See Figure 25.2 for how it works.

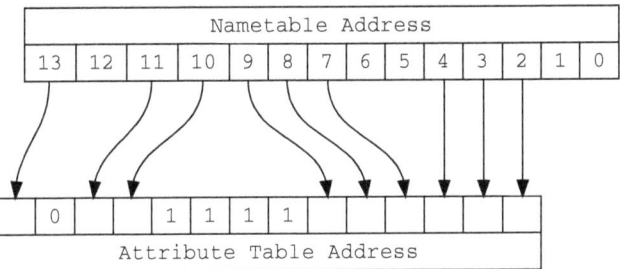

Figure 25.2: Converting nametable address to attribute table address.

Now we have to write the stack of attribute table entries to the VRAM buffer. We can't use the VRAMBUF_VERT option, because each row is eight bytes long, not 32 bytes like the nametable. So we make a new **put_attr_entries()** function that writes each byte individually:

```
void put_attr_entries(word addr) {
  byte i;
  for (i=0; i<PLAYROWS/4; i++) {
    VRAMBUF_PUT(addr, attrbuf[i], 0);
    addr += 8;
  }
  vrambuf_end();
}
```

The VRAMBUF_PUT macro adds a packet to the VRAM buffer that writes a single byte to video RAM at a particular address.

25. Offscreen Scrolling

In **update_offscreen()**, we call **nt2attraddr()** to get the attribute table address, then pass this value to **put_attr_entries()**:

```
put_attr_entries(nt2attraddr(addr));
```

We update the attribute table every two columns. Every four columns, we clear it:

```
// every 4 columns, clear attribute table buffer
if ((x & 3) == 2) {
  memset(attrbuf, 0, sizeof(attrbuf));
}
```

This allows us to set the leftmost attribute table entries first, then OR them with the rightmost entries later. This prevents color artifacts from showing on the right edge of the screen, since we update so close to the edge. (We could avoid this by just drawing a little further off-screen.)

Now that we're done with this stack of metatiles, we decrement the seg_width variable. When it decrements to zero, we randomly generate another segment with **new_segment()**:

```
if (--seg_width == 0) {
  new_segment();
}
```

25.5 The Main Loop

Now that we've defined all of these functions, we'll put it all together in a main loop.

We'll first define a **scroll_left()** function that scrolls one pixel to the left. We first check to see if 16 pixels have scrolled by. If so, we call **update_offscreen()**:

```
void scroll_left() {
  // update nametable every 16 pixels
  if ((x_scroll & 15) == 0) {
    update_offscreen();
  }
  // increment x_scroll
  ++x_scroll;
}
```

Our main loop for this demo is an infinite **while** loop. On each loop iteration, it dumps the VRAM buffer to video RAM, splits the screen, and then calls **scroll_left()**.

```
while (1) {
  // ensure VRAM buffer is cleared
  ppu_wait_nmi();
  vrambuf_clear();
  // split at x_scroll
  split(x_scroll, 0);
  // scroll to the left
  scroll_left();
}
```

We should clear the VRAM buffer on every frame. The safest time to do this is right after the NMI interrupt flushes out the previous updates to the PPU. This is why we call **ppu_wait_nmi()** and then **vrambuf_clear()** immediately afterward.

> ❶ You can display all four nametables at once in the **8bitworkshop IDE**. Click the NES emulator display and type **Ctrl+Alt+Shift+N**.

25.6 Alternate Methods

This demo randomly generates each segment of the game world. If we wanted to design our levels ahead of time, it wouldn't be a big change. We would just store a list of segments in PRG ROM, fetching each one in turn as we render new portions of the level offscreen.

Some games store the entire nametable and attribute table for each screen of the level. Each screen takes 1024 bytes, so we'd want to use some sort of *compression* method to reduce the size of the level in ROM. You would need to split screens into slices, as there isn't enough CPU time to decompress and write an entire screen to video RAM during a NMI period.

There's no requirement that we only draw one stack of metatiles at a time. We could even update the entire offscreen portion at

25. Offscreen Scrolling

once, but we don't have much time during the vertical blank period. NESLib can only write about 140 bytes per frame using its VRAM buffer method. So our compression method would have to operate on slices — vertical columns like this example, or horizontal slices if we were scrolling vertically.

We could even modify this example to use horizontal mirroring, allowing us to also scroll vertically between two complete screens. If the PPU_MASK is set to mask the leftmost eight pixels, we won't see the updates. We'd have to write only one column of tiles at a time instead of two. You can change the NES_MIRRORING variable to 0 and experiment.

> Can you add a player metasprite based on the code in Chapter 13: Controllers?
>
> How would you detect collisions between the player and the metatiles? How would you model gravity and make the player jump?
>
> Can you scroll the screen in the other direction? Why or why not? Would it make a difference if the level was stored in ROM and not randomly generated?

26

Main Loop vs. NMI Handler

For any given function in a NES program, there is a choice of where to place it — in the *main loop*, or in the *NMI handler*.

The NMI handler runs 60 times per second, which makes it a useful place to put things that run every frame, like music and sound updates, controller polling, and so on. It's also invaluable for writing to the PPU during the vertical blank period.

The main loop refers to the code outside of the interrupt handler(s). It's not automatically synced to the video frame (though you can wait for events), so you can write code that crosses frame boundaries.

NESLib is set up to do most PPU and video RAM updates in the NMI handler. In this scheme, the main loop can safely do these things:

- Game logic.
- Manipulate the OAM (sprite) buffer. NESLib copies the OAM buffer to the PPU in the NMI handler.
- Fill the VRAM buffer, like in Chapter 14. NESLib copies this to video RAM in the NMI handler.
- Call NESLib functions to do palette updates, scrolling, PPU control and mask changes. The changes are buffered internally and applied in the next NMI handler.
- APU updates, unless this is done in the NMI handler.

26. Main Loop vs. NMI Handler

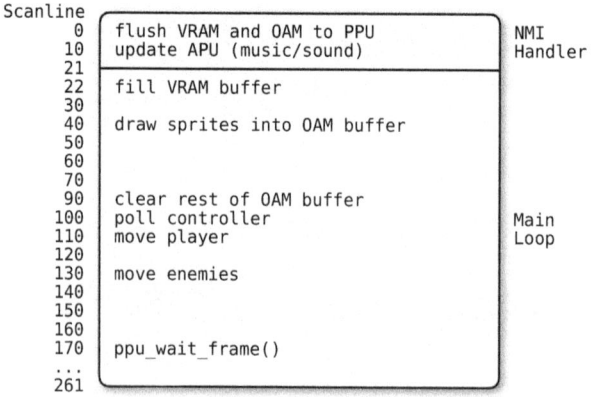

Figure 26.1: Example frame budget for a NES game

If you share PPU updates between your NMI handler and main loop, they can conflict. For example, if an interrupt occurs in the main loop while writing data to video RAM, the interrupt handler could change the PPU address, corrupting the main loop's write.

There are some situations where you have to talk to the PPU in the main loop, like when performing a *screen split*. If the split is near the top of the screen, like when doing a status bar, you could put the split at the end of the NMI handler without losing too many cycles.

When using assembler, there are other ways to structure your code. You could put all of the code in the NMI handler, replacing your main loop with an infinite empty loop. Many commercial NES games work this way. You'd have to be careful that the NMI handler doesn't run long, though, since another NMI could fire and start filling up the stack.

You could also put all of the code in the main loop. You'd still need the NMI handler to increment a counter, which the main loop could poll to see when vertical blank has started. It could then issue PPU updates. However, you'd have to poll quite often to avoid missing your update window.

27

Climber: Platform Game

> Open the example on 8bitworkshop.com: From the **Platforms** menu, select **Game Consoles » NES**, then select the **Climber Game** project from the Project Selector dropdown.

We've distilled the concepts from previous chapters into *Climber*, a small platform game. You run, jump, and climb ladders, avoiding enemies and collecting items. Each level is randomly generated; the goal is to climb to the top.

27. Climber: Platform Game

27.1 Modeling The Game World

When starting to program a game, we'll often think not only about what code to write, but which data structures best represent the state of the game world.

The world of *Climber* is a randomly-generated building with many floors of varying heights. (In the terminology of Chapter 25, each floor is a *segment*.)

Each floor has ladders between them, items, and gaps the player can fall through. We use the **typedef** and **struct** keywords to define a C *struct* type that holds the various attributes:

```
typedef struct Floor {
  byte ypos;          // # of tiles from ground
  int height:4;       // # of tiles to next floor
  int gap:4;          // X position of gap
  int ladder1:4;      // X position of first ladder
  int ladder2:4;      // X position of second ladder
  int objtype:4;      // item type (FloorItem)
  int objpos:4;       // X position of object
} Floor;
```

You may notice the :4 suffix on some int fields. This is called a *bitfield*. We ask the compiler to pack each field above into four bits, except for ypos, which takes eight bits. This reduces the size of a *struct* and saves memory.

You can guess the final struct size by adding the bit lengths: $8 + 4 * 6 = 32$, or 4 bytes. If we didn't use bitfields, the struct would be at least seven bytes.

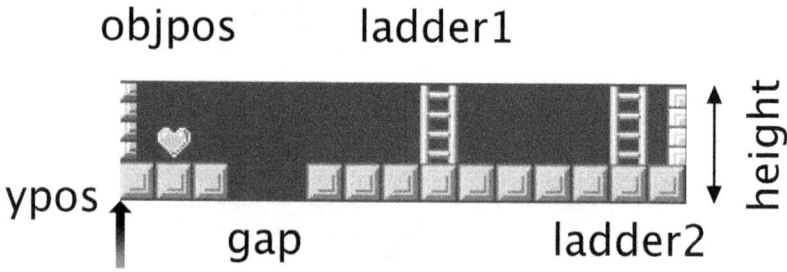

Figure 27.1: Attributes of a floor structure.

We also use an **enum** to define the types of items the player can pick up.

```
typedef enum FloorItem { ITEM_NONE, ITEM_MINE, ITEM_HEART,
    ITEM_POWER };
```

The **enum** keyword assigns increasing numeric values to identifiers. In this example, ITEM_NONE is 0, ITEM_MINE is 1, and so forth.

We can make an array of Floor structs, one entry per floor:

```
Floor floors[MAX_FLOORS];
```

It's preferable that each Floor struct is four bytes — a *power of two*. This allows array calculations to be fast, since the compiler can multiply by four by shifting left twice.

> The 6502 can't access structs very efficiently. If we were writing this code in assembler, we would probably use multiple byte arrays (one per attribute) instead of an array of structs.

27.2 Generating The Game World

When we start a game level, we randomly generate the list of floors via the **make_floors()** function:

```
for (i=0; i<MAX_FLOORS; i++) {
  Floor* lev = &floors[i];
  // ... set floor attributes ...
  y += lev->height;
}
```

In each loop iteration, we compute a *pointer* to each Floor structure in the array. This allows us to modify structure fields through the pointer using the -> operator.

We use our **rndint()** function developed in Chapter 16 to generate random numbers. For example, each floor can be four, six, or eight tiles high:

```
lev->height = rndint(2,5)*2;
```

We don't allow floor heights to be odd numbers because the attribute table works on 2x2 tile blocks.

Some of the floor attributes depend on other attributes, sometimes on the previous floor. For example, we don't want ladders to end up in a gap on the floor above. The gap attribute defines the X coordinate of the left side of the gap in the floor. While generating gaps, we look to see if it intersects ladders on the floor below, and if so we grab another random number:

```
do {
  // only have gaps in floors 5 and above
  lev->gap = i>=5 ? rndint(0,13) : 0;
} while (ladder_in_gap(prevlev->ladder1, lev->gap) ||
         ladder_in_gap(prevlev->ladder2, lev->gap));
```

The roof of the building is the player's goal. We'll make it the maximum height, and have no items, gaps, or ladders. So we should just see open sky above.

```
floors[MAX_FLOORS-1].height = 15;
floors[MAX_FLOORS-1].gap = 0;
floors[MAX_FLOORS-1].ladder1 = 0;
floors[MAX_FLOORS-1].ladder2 = 0;
floors[MAX_FLOORS-1].objtype = 0;
```

27.3 Drawing the Game World

We implemented a demo in Chapter 25 that scrolled horizontally in one direction. We generated new buildings continuously, only worrying about the current building that was drawn offscreen.

Climber will feature a vertically scrolling game world, but will allow the player to move up and down, revisiting previous floors. So the draw function will be a little more complicated.

Our main background drawing routine is **draw_floor_line()**. Its sole argument is row_height, the row to draw relative to the bottom of the level. So 0 is the lowest row, 1 the one above it, and so on.

27.3. Drawing the Game World

```
// draw a nametable line into the frame buffer at <row_height>
// 0 == bottom of stage
void draw_floor_line(byte row_height) {
```

The outer loop of this function iterates through all of the floors in the level. For each floor, we calculate dy, the row relative to the floor. When we find a floor that intersects row_height, we draw the row, then use the **break** keyword to exit the loop:

```
  for (floor=0; floor<MAX_FLOORS; floor++) {
    Floor* lev = &floors[floor];
    // compute height in rows above floor
    byte dy = row_height - lev->ypos;
    // does this floor intersect the desired row?
    if (dy < lev->height) {
      // ...... draw row at the given height ......
      break; // break out of loop
    }
  }
}
```

dy tells us the distance in tiles from the floor's bottom, which determines what to draw. The first two rows (dy < 2) are pretty easy. They're just 2x2 metatiles, and an optional gap of blank spaces. We draw into buf, our 32-byte buffer:

```
    // iterate through all 32 columns
    for (i=0; i<COLS; i+=2) {
      if (dy) {
        buf[i]   = CH_FLOOR;      // upper-left
        buf[i+1] = CH_FLOOR+2;    // upper-right
      } else {
        buf[i]   = CH_FLOOR+1;    // lower-left
        buf[i+1] = CH_FLOOR+3;    // lower-right
      }
    }
    if (lev->gap)                 // is there a gap?
      memset(buf+lev->gap*2, 0, GAPSIZE); // clear gap
```

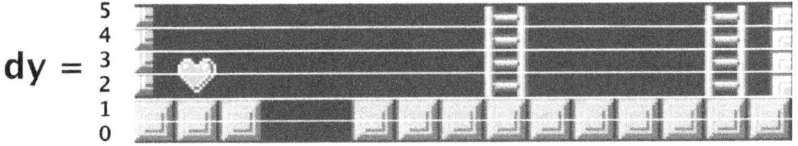

135

27. Climber: Platform Game

Above the floor of the floor (dy >= 2), it gets a little more complex. Most of it is empty space, but there are walls on either side and up to 2 ladders:

```
memset(buf, 0, sizeof(buf));         // clear buffer
if (floor < MAX_FLOORS-1) {          // draw walls?
  buf[0] = CH_FLOOR+1;               // left side
  buf[COLS-1] = CH_FLOOR;            // right side
}
if (lev->ladder1) {                  // draw ladder 1?
  buf[lev->ladder1*2] = CH_LADDER;         // left
  buf[lev->ladder1*2+1] = CH_LADDER+1;     // right
}
if (lev->ladder2) {                  // draw ladder 2?
  buf[lev->ladder2*2] = CH_LADDER;         // left
  buf[lev->ladder2*2+1] = CH_LADDER+1;     // right
}
```

Floors may have an optional item on rows 2 and 3, if `objtype` is non-zero. These are 2x2 metatiles:

```
if (lev->objtype) {                  // draw object?
  byte ch = lev->objtype*4 + CH_ITEM; // which pattern?
  if (dy == 2) {
    buf[lev->objpos*2] = ch+1;       // bottom-left
    buf[lev->objpos*2+1] = ch+3;     // bottom-right
  }
  else if (dy == 3) {
    buf[lev->objpos*2] = ch+0;       // top-left
    buf[lev->objpos*2+1] = ch+2;     // top-right
  }
}
```

Now that our `buf` is full of tile data for a row, we have to figure out where in video RAM to write it. Each nametable is 30 rows high, so two nametables stacked atop each other are 60 rows tall. The row number wraps around the nametables, as shown in Figure 27.2.

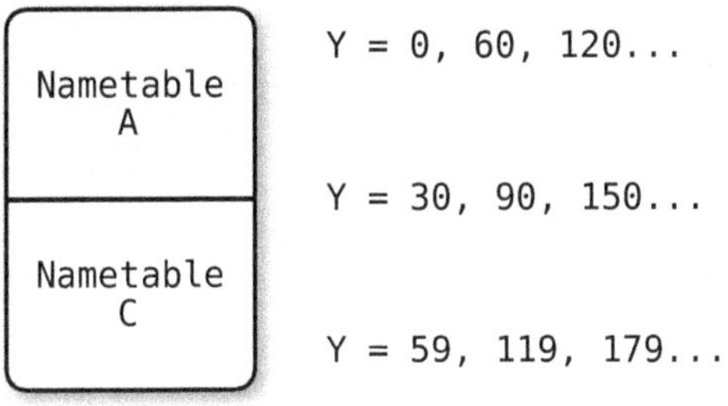

27.3. Drawing the Game World

```
              Y = 0, 60, 120...
  Nametable
      A
              Y = 30, 90, 150...
  Nametable
      C
              Y = 59, 119, 179...
```

Figure 27.2: Visualization of getntaddr() function.

As we ascend and descend the level, we always write a row offscreen. We use the *modulo* operator to force the row number into the range 0 to 59, ensuring it wraps around to the other side as we scroll upward and downward:

```
// compute row in name buffer and address (ROWS is 60)
rowy = (ROWS-1) - (screen_y % ROWS);
addr = getntaddr(1, rowy);
```

Since we're scrolling between nametables A and C, our target address can be in either nametable. The **getntaddr()** function looks at the Y parameter and figures this out:

```
word getntaddr(byte x, byte y) {
  word addr;
  if (y < 30) {
    addr = NTADR_A(x,y);
  } else {
    addr = NTADR_C(x,y-30);
  }
  return addr;
}
```

Now we just write the final row to the target address using the *VRAM buffer* routines:

```
// copy line to screen buffer
vrambuf_put(addr, buf, COLS);
```

We also have to also write to the *attribute table* every four rows, because attribute table entries handle a 4x4 grid of tiles. We want to make the first two rows of a floor have a different palette than the others.

The attribute byte depends on whether the floor aligns with the top or bottom of the 4x4 attribute block:

```
if ((addr & 0x60) == 0) {    // is this row a multiple of 4?
  byte a;
  if (dy==1)      a = 0x05;  // top of attribute block
  else if (dy==3) a = 0x50;  // bottom of attribute block
  else            a = 0x00;  // does not intersect attr. block
  memset(attrs, a, 8);       // set entire row with same byte
  vrambuf_put(nt2attraddr(addr), attrs, 8);    // write row
}
```

Note that we use the **nt2attraddr()** function to compute the address in the attribute table, described in Chapter 25.

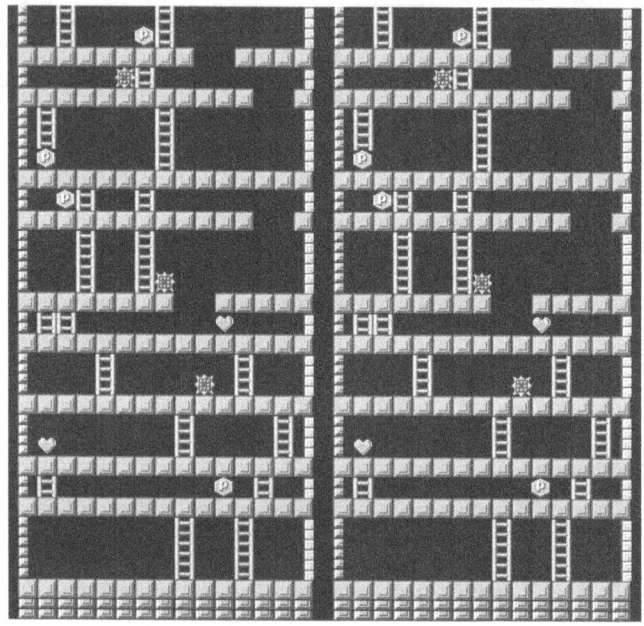

Figure 27.3: Climber game nametables, with horizontal mirroring

27.4 Scrolling the Game World

Now we have all the elements necessary to draw and scroll the game world.

We maintain two different variables which represent the current scrolled position of the world.

27.4. Scrolling the Game World

```
// 16-bit vertical scroll amount in pixels/scanlines
static int scroll_pixel_yy = 0;

// 8-bit vertical scroll amount in tiles
static byte scroll_tile_y = 0;
```

When the level starts, we set the scroll position to 0:

```
set_scroll_pixel_yy(0);
```

The **set_scroll_pixel_yy()** computes the new scroll register values:

```
scroll_pixel_yy = yy;        // get scroll pos. in pixels
scroll_tile_y = yy >> 3;     // divide by 8
scroll(0, 479 - ((yy + 224) % 480));
```

Note that we again use the *modulo* operator to force the Y scroll register into the range 0 through 479. It will wrap around as we scroll upward and downward.

The function also draws a new row of tiles offscreen whenever we scroll eight pixels. Depending on whether we're scrolling up or down, it'll either draw the row above (+30) or below (-30) the visible screen. The nametable address will be the same in each case, even though different parts of the level are drawn.

```
if ((yy & 7) == 0) {
  // scrolling upward or downward?
  if (yy > scroll_pixel_yy)
    draw_floor_line(scroll_tile_y + 30);    // above
  else
    draw_floor_line(scroll_tile_y - 30);    // below
}
```

We also need to redraw when the player picks up an item. Items are 2x2 tiles, so we can just redraw the third and fourth rows, which contain the item:

```
void refresh_floor(byte floor) {
  byte y = floors[floor].ypos;   // get floor bottom coordinate
  draw_floor_line(y+2);          // redraw 3rd line
  draw_floor_line(y+3);          // redraw 4th line
}
```

That's how we draw the game world into the background layer. Now, let's talk about moving objects.

27.5 Actors

Arcade games usually have objects that move around the game world and interact. We'll call these objects *actors*, and the player is one of them.

We've got three types of actors: The player, the enemies, and the rescuee at the top of the building. We'll define them in an **enum**:

```
typedef enum ActorType {
  ACTOR_PLAYER, ACTOR_ENEMY, ACTOR_RESCUE};
```

Actors can run, climb, jump, fall, or just stand still:

```
typedef enum ActorState {
  INACTIVE, STANDING, WALKING, CLIMBING, JUMPING, FALLING,
    PACING};
```

PACING is a special state reserved for the rescuee at the top of the building. (Because we're lazy, this actor doesn't really pace, it just stands still.)

```
typedef struct Actor {
  word yy;           // Y position in pixels (16 bit)
  byte x;            // X position in pixels (8 bit)
  byte floor;        // floor index
  byte state;        // ActorState
  int name:2;        // ActorType (2 bits)
  int pal:2;         // palette color (2 bits)
  int dir:1;         // direction (0=right, 1=left)
  int onscreen:1;    // is actor onscreen?
  sbyte yvel;        // Y velocity
  sbyte xvel;        // X velocity
} Actor;
```

The yy field is 16 bits wide, and contains the scroll-independent vertical position of the player. It describes the distances to the bottom of the building in pixels.

The x field is only eight bits wide, since we don't scroll horizontally in this game.

The floor field changes when the actor goes up or down a level. This makes it easier to find ladders, items, and collisions with other actors.

Note again the use of *bitfields* in this struct. All of the bitfields sum to 8, meaning they all fit in a single byte. The total struct size is 8 bytes, which is a power-of-two so access will be faster.

27.6 The Player

When we start a level, we zero out the actors array, then create the player's actor. The player is always at actor index 0:

```
memset(actors, 0, sizeof(actors));
actors[0].state = STANDING;
actors[0].name = ACTOR_PLAYER;
actors[0].pal = 3;
actors[0].x = 64;
actors[0].floor = 0;
actors[0].yy = get_floor_yy(0);
```

The **get_floor_yy()** function returns a 16-bit position representing the distance in pixels from the bottom of a floor to the bottom of the building. We use that to position our player at the bottom floor.

To scroll, we call **check_scroll_up()** and **check_scroll_down()** whenever we move the player. If player_screen_y goes too far up or down, we scroll the screen with **set_scroll_pixel_yy()**.

```
void check_scroll_up() {
  if (player_screen_y < ACTOR_SCROLL_UP_Y)
    set_scroll_pixel_yy(scroll_pixel_yy + 1);   // scroll up
}
void check_scroll_down() {
  if (player_screen_y > ACTOR_SCROLL_DOWN_Y &&
      scroll_pixel_yy>0)
    set_scroll_pixel_yy(scroll_pixel_yy - 1);   // scroll down
}
```

We only call these when the player is in certain states — for example, we don't want to scroll the screen in JUMPING state, because this would move the screen up and down unnecessarily.

27.7 Vanishing and Reappearing Actors

We'd like our scrolling world to contain dozens of enemies. Since most are offscreen at any given time, we don't want to waste CPU time moving them. We don't have enough hardware sprites to display them all at once, either.

Our approach is to create enemies on-demand, when the player scrolls to a new region of the level. Whenever we draw a floor to video memory, we also see if we need to create an actor:

```
// create actors on this floor, if needed
if (dy == 0 && (floor >= 2)) {
  create_actors_on_floor(floor);
}
```

Each floor spawns one enemy. There are more floors than actors, so multiple floors map to a given actor slot.

```
byte actor_index = (floor_index % (MAX_ACTORS-1)) + 1;
```

We'll only replace the existing actor in this slot if it has been tagged as offscreen (the player never should go offscreen, since the level scrolls with them):

```
struct Actor* a = &actors[actor_index];
if (!a->onscreen) {
  ... create actor ...
}
```

We set the actor's default attributes — standing on the given floor, with a random X position. We then set its `onscreen` field to 1:

```
Floor *floor = &floors[floor_index];
a->state = STANDING;
a->name = ACTOR_ENEMY;
a->x = rand8();
a->yy = get_floor_yy(floor_index);
a->floor = floor_index;
a->onscreen = 1;
```

There's a special case for the rescuee on the roof. We set a special sprite, set position all the way left, change the color, and use the `PACING` actor state.

```
// rescue person on top of the building
if (floor_index == MAX_FLOORS-1) {
  a->name = ACTOR_RESCUE;
  a->state = PACING;
  a->x = 0;
  a->pal = 1;
}
```

27.8 Drawing Actors

Drawing an individual actor is done in **draw_actor()**. First, we get a pointer to the Actor structure and define some local variables:

```
void draw_actor(byte i) {
  struct Actor* a = &actors[i];   // pointer to Actor
  bool dir;                       // true=left, false=right
  const unsigned char* meta;      // metasprite pointer
  byte x,y;                       // X and Y coordinates
```

We compute the Y position of the actor relative to the scroll position:

```
  int screen_y = SCREEN_Y_BOTTOM - a->yy + scroll_pixel_yy;
```

If the actor is sufficiently offscreen, we set its offscreen field to zero. This allows it to be reused by another actor (or the same one, if the screen scrolls in their direction again).

```
  if (screen_y > 192+8 || screen_y < -18) {
    a->onscreen = 0;              // offscreen vertically
    return;
  }
```

Then we select which *metasprite* definition to use for the actor. We'll use the **switch** keyword to choose different code statements based on the actor's state:

```
  switch (a->state) {
    case STANDING: // set metasprite for standing up
    case WALKING:  // set metasprite for walking animation
  }
```

27. Climber: Platform Game

We'll write different **case** statements for each actor state. For example, when STANDING we choose between left and write standing sprites based on the actor's direction:

```
case STANDING:
  meta = dir ? playerLStand : playerRStand;
  break; // exit switch statement
```

For WALKING, we animate between multiple sprites based on the X position and the direction facing:

```
case WALKING:
  meta = playerRunSeq[((a->x >> 1) & 7) + (dir?0:8)];
  break;
}
```

Now we call **oam_meta_spr_pal()** to draw the metasprite, also passing the palette index of the actor:

```
x = a->x;
y = screen_y;
oam_meta_spr_pal(x, y, a->pal, meta);
```

This function will update the global oam_off variable.

Before returning, we make sure to set this actor's onscreen field to 1:

```
a->onscreen = 1;
```

We draw all sprites in the **refresh_sprites()** function. We're using NESLib's built-in global oam_off variable, so we don't have to pass oam_id around.

```
void refresh_sprites() {
  byte i;
  oam_off = 0;                  // reset sprite index to 0
  for (i=0; i<MAX_ACTORS; i++)
    draw_actor(i);              // draw each actor
  draw_scoreboard();            // draw scoreboard
  oam_hide_rest(oam_off);       // hide rest of actors
}
```

27.9 Scoreboard

Since this is a vertically scrolling game, drawing a status bar is difficult. It's pretty easy to use two hardware sprites for a simple score display, though. We could get fancier, but then we'd reduce the number of sprites available for actors.

```
void draw_scoreboard() {
  oam_off = oam_spr(24+0, 24, '0'+(score >> 4), 2, oam_off);
  oam_off = oam_spr(24+8, 24, '0'+(score & 0xf), 2, oam_off);
}
```

27.10 Checking Collisions

The NES can only check sprite zero for collisions against the background, so it's not useful for checking collisions between sprites.

This is an expensive function, as it must iterate through the entire list of actors. We only need to check against the player, so we only need to iterate once. We speed it up a bit by only allowing collisions of actors on the same floor — we can check each actor's floor field.

```
bool check_collision(Actor* a) {
  byte i;
  byte afloor = a->floor;
  if (afloor == 0) return false;     // can't fall thru basement
  if (a->state == FALLING) return false;   // already falling
  for (i=1; i<MAX_ACTORS; i++) {     // iterate list of actors
    Actor* b = &actors[i];
    if (b->onscreen &&               // actor must be visible
        afloor == b->floor &&        // ... on the same floor
        iabs(a->yy - b->yy) < 8 &&   // ... within 8 pixels
        iabs(a->x - b->x) < 8) {     // ... on X and Y axes
      return true;                   // collision found
    }
  }
  return false;                      // no collision
}
```

27.11 The Main Game Loop

We repeat this loop until the player reaches the top floor:

```
while (actors[0].floor != MAX_FLOORS-1) {
  ... draw one frame, move actors ...
}
```

First, we call **vrambuf_flush()** to flush the VRAM buffer and wait for *VBLANK*. Then we call **refresh_sprites()** to draw actors and the scoreboard.

```
vrambuf_flush();     // wait for vsync, flush buffer to VRAM
refresh_sprites();                       // redraw sprites
move_player();              // move player via controller
```

move_player() reads controllers and moves the player, which in turn calls **move_actor()**.

```
void move_player() {
  byte joy = pad_poll(0);                // read controller
  move_actor(&actors[0], joy, true);         // move player
  pickup_object(&actors[0]);     // pickup object on floor?
}
```

What about moving the enemies? This is the fun part. Enemy actors follow the same rules as the player — they run, jump, climb, and fall. So for each enemy actor, we just pass a random input to **move_actor()**!

```
for (i=1; i<MAX_ACTORS; i++) {
  move_actor(&actors[i], rand8(), false); // move randomly
}
```

Now we check to see if the player hit another actor:

```
if (check_collision(&actors[0])) {         // collision?
  fall_down(&actors[0]);            // player falls down
  sfx_play(SND_HIT,0);                 // play a sound
  vbright = 8;                     // flash the screen
}
```

Note that we set vbright to flash the screen white. We'll count it down each frame until it gets back to 4 (normal brightness):

```
if (vbright > 4) {
  pal_bright(--vbright);
}
```

27.12 Level Win Animation

When we get to the top, we want a little animation to reward the player! When the player's floor reaches MAX_FLOORS-1, we call the **rescue_scene()** function. It faces the player to the left, then types a little message to the player.

type_message() writes each character of a message to the nametable, waiting a few frames between each letter. It uses scroll_tile_y to figure out the initial row of the message, a few frames above the roof.

27.13 Music, Sound, and main()

We use the *FamiTone2* library to render music and sound effects:

```
void setup_sounds() {
  famitone_init(danger_streets_music_data);
  sfx_init(demo_sounds);
  nmi_set_callback(famitone_update);
}
```

When we want to play a sound effect:

```
    sfx_play(SND_START,0);
```

Now that we have all the pieces, our **main()** function is pretty simple. We set up the sound/music engine, set up graphics and the PPU, and make a random set of floors. Then we call **play_scene()** to play the game.

```
void main() {
  setup_sounds();              // init famitone library
  while (1) {
    setup_graphics();          // setup PPU, clear screen
    sfx_play(SND_START,0);     // play starting sound
    make_floors();             // make random level
    music_play(0);             // start the music
    play_scene();              // play the level
  }
}
```

27. Climber: Platform Game

 What would you do to improve this game? Different floor types? Better enemy AI? Player special moves and attacks? Elevators? See if you can hack on the code and come up with a better version!

28

Advanced Mappers

In Chapter 10, we discussed horizontal and vertical mirroring, which are different modes that are influenced by scroll direction. This is just one NES function influenced by the mapper. *Mapper* is a broad term referring to the various circuits and hardware inside of the cartridge that extend the console's functionality, apart from the program and graphics ROM.

Mappers are usually tailored to a specific game. Emulator authors and enthusiasts have reverse-engineered most of the mappers "in the wild" and have come up with a taxonomy of sorts. Each mapper has a special code in the *iNES header* that tells the emulator how to simulate the mapper circuitry. There are hundreds of different types of mappers, but in this book we're going to cover the most popular ones used by homebrew authors.

You may also want to refer to the NES Architecture Diagram in Figure 5.2 on page 25.

28.1 Cartridge Connector

The functionality of a mapper is limited to what is exposed by the *cartridge connector*, a 72-pin connector on the NES. Both the CPU and PPU buses go through the connector. This allows the mapper to intercept the signals and respond to memory reads and writes.

28. Advanced Mappers

28.2 Bank Switching

The default NES memory map can only address 32 KB of PRG ROM for program code. Many cartridges expand this by implementing a *bank switching* scheme.

The ROM is partitioned into several sections, called *banks*. By writing to mapper-specific registers, the program can swap them in and out of address space when needed.

Bank switching schemes vary; there may be fixed banks that cannot be swapped, there may be variable-sized banks, and there may be limitations on which banks can be swapped into which memory regions.

The *CHR ROM* can also be bank switched. The PPU can only see 8 KB (512 tiles) at once, but with clever screen-splitting, you can swap banks while the frame is being drawn, showing more tiles in a frame.

We'll go over a specific bank switching scheme in Chapter 30.

28.3 CHR ROM vs. CHR RAM

An NES cartridge contains at least two chips — one *PRG ROM* (program code, connected to the CPU) and one *CHR ROM* (pattern tables, connected to the PPU). Some cartridges replace CHR ROM with a *CHR RAM* chip.

This allows more flexibility, since the pattern tables can be created dynamically via the CPU. If compression techniques are used, this can reduce the total ROM space needed. In Chapter 29, we'll go over some CHR RAM applications in more detail.

28.4 Extra or battery-backed RAM

Many cartridges have an 8 KB PRG RAM region at $6000-$7FFF accessible by the CPU. Sometimes this is protected by a battery so that it persists when the cartridge loses power, and is used for save game data. Otherwise, it is used for extra temporary working RAM for the CPU.

28.5 Interrupts

We already discussed the NMI, which occurs once per video frame. This is built into the NES, and cannot be changed by the mapper.

The 6502 also supports an *IRQ*, or *interrupt request* signal. This can be triggered by the mapper, and is often used to count scanlines for *screen split*s or other special effects.

We'll explore this feature in Chapter 31.

28.6 Expansion Audio

The cartridge connector also has a pass-through for audio output from the *APU (Audio Processing Unit)*. The mapper can alter this to add custom sound effects or extra sound channels, or even FM synthesis music.

28.7 Fast Multiplication

The 6502 doesn't have a multiplication or division instruction, so these operations must be done via software. This is much slower than addition or subtraction. To make it faster, some mappers like *MMC5* have a *hardware multiplication* circuit which multiplies two 8-bit numbers into a 16-bit register.

28.8 Advanced Mirroring

As we learned in Chapter 10, the NES has four logical nametables, but only enough RAM for two physical nametables. The other two nametables are *mirrored* horizontally or vertically.

This setting is controlled by the mapper. The A10 line of the cartridge connector is connected to the PPU's A10 for vertical mirroring, or the PPU's A11 for horizontal mirroring. Some mappers set this with a software switch so it can change at runtime.

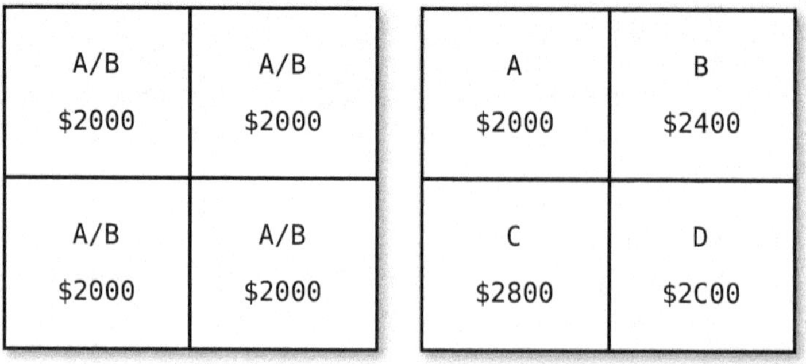

28. Advanced Mappers

A/B	A/B		A	B
$2000	$2000		$2000	$2400
A/B	A/B		C	D
$2000	$2000		$2800	$2C00

Figure 28.1: Single-screen (left) and four-screen (right) mirroring.

Some mappers implement *single-screen mirroring*. There are still two nametables, A and B, but only one of them can be active at a time. The active nametable is mirrored in all directions.

This makes displaying a status bar easy, since you can just flip to the other nametable at the split. Glitches can be a problem when scrolling, since there is no offscreen region to draw into. When scrolling vertically, glitches can be hidden behind the status bar.

Some cartridges add additional nametable RAM to implement *four-screen mirroring*. This creates a full 64x60 tilemap, allowing horizontal and vertical scrolling in any direction without glitching.

More exotic setups are possible, like diagonal or L-shaped mirroring. The **JSNES** emulator in the IDE only supports horizontal, vertical, and single-screen mirroring.

29
CHR RAM

We've been using *CHR ROM* in all of the previous examples, which limits us to one or more fixed pattern tables for the entire game.

Sometimes, though, it's useful to use RAM for the pattern tables. Instead of being limited to fixed pattern tables, we can modify them at runtime.

The **8bitworkshop IDE** lets you change *iNES header* parameters using C *preprocessor defines*. (We'll discuss the iNES header in more detail in Chapter 34.) The following lines set up our build to use *CHR RAM*:

```
#define NES_MAPPER 2     // mapper 2 (UxROM mapper)
#define NES_CHR_BANKS 0  // CHR RAM
```

This lets us use a different *mapper*. Our previous examples used mapper 0, also named *NROM* – a very simple mapper that uses CHR and PRG ROM. To use CHR RAM, we tell the linker to use mapper 2 (*UxROM*) and set the number of CHR ROM banks to zero.

Before we enable the PPU, we should copy our default pattern tables to video RAM. This is just like writing to the nametable or any other PPU memory, using the **vram_adr()** and **vram_write()** functions.

29. CHR RAM

For example:

```
// copy background tiles
vram_adr(0x0);
vram_write(BG_TILES, sizeof(BG_TILES));
// copy sprite tiles
vram_adr(0x1000);
vram_write(SPR_TILES, sizeof(SPR_TILES));
```

In the *Solarian* game, we use CHR RAM to generate eight different copies of the enemy sprites, each shifted by one pixel, using the **set_shifted_pattern()** function. Then, we can use background tiles to show enemies in formation, moving them left and right by switching them to different pixel-aligned copies. We convert enemies to sprites when they descend to attack the player's ship.

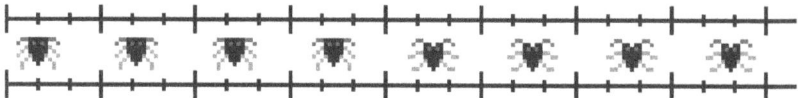

Figure 29.1: 24x8 pixel sprites, each successively shifted by one pixel. Some of the shapes are different, which creates animation as they move.

29.1 Monochrome 1bpp Frame Buffer

With some clever programming, we can trick the NES into thinking it has a 256x240 *frame buffer*. This allows us to draw pixels anywhere on the screen — slowly, and limited to one color plus the background.

We split the screen into four equal sections, as shown in Figure 29.2. Each section displays a unique bitmap. This requires a couple of tricks.

29.1. Monochrome 1bpp Frame Buffer

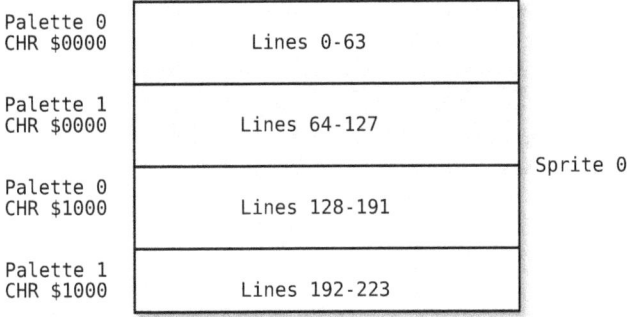

Figure 29.2: Sections for monochrome 1bpp mode

You may notice that the first and third sections share the same CHR RAM range as the second and fourth. They should show the same bitmaps — but they don't because they're mapped to different palettes. The palettes are specifically chosen so that only one bit of the pattern table is significant. This essentially turns the 2-bit tile patterns into two 1-bit patterns.

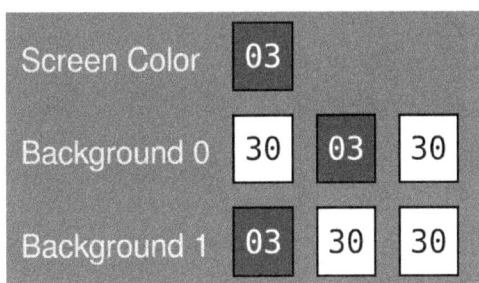

Figure 29.3: Palette for monochrome 1bpp mode

The bottom two sections are just like the top two, except they use the second pattern table.

Our nametable is just the sequence of bytes from 0 to 255. This way, we cover the entire range of patterns for each of the four sections.

29. CHR RAM

```
$2000   $00 $01 $02 $03 $04 $05 $06 $07 ... $1F
$2020   $20 $21 $22 $23 $24 $25 $26 $27 ... $3F
$2040   $40 $41 $42 $43 $44 $45 $46 $47 ... $5F
$2060   $60 $61 $62 $63 $64 $65 $66 $67 ... $7F
$2080   $80 $81 $82 $83 $84 $85 $86 $87 ... $9F
$20A0   $A0 $A1 $A2 $A3 $A4 $A5 $A6 $A7 ... $BF
$20C0   $C0 $C1 $C2 $C3 $C4 $C5 $C6 $C7 ... $DF
$20E0   $E0 $E1 $E2 $E3 $E4 $E5 $E6 $E7 ... $FF
```

Figure 29.4: Name table layout of monochrome 1bpp mode

We'll use a *sprite zero* split (as discussed in Chapter 15) to switch between the pattern tables. We have to call **split()** every frame, then immediately afterward switch to CHR bank 1. NESLib will reset the CHR bank to 0 on the next NMI.

```
while (!done) {
  ppu_wait_nmi();
  monobitmap_split();
}
```

The **monobitmap_split()** has to have precise timing — not the thing C is known for! We have to call **split()**, then set the PPU control register at exactly the right time:

```
void monobitmap_split() {
  // split screen at line 128
  split(0,0);
  DELAYLOOP(15); // delay until end of line
  PPU.control = PPU.control ^ 0x10; // bg bank 1
}
```

Changing the CHR bank during a scanline requires precise timing. We have to set the PPU control register between pixel 257 and 320 of the current scanline. DELAYLOOP is a little *inline assembly* macro that delays the CPU a few cycles to get into this range. We'll explain more about scanline timing in Chapter 41.

Drawing pixels is a little non-intuitive. For each pixel, we must determine its section (of the four main sections), its tile (of the 256 tiles) and its bitplane (of the two bitplanes per tile).

29.1. Monochrome 1bpp Frame Buffer

This shows how pixels are ordered in pattern table RAM:

```
X:            0         8        16        24       32
Line 0     | $0000    $0008    $0010    $0018   | ...
Line 1     | $0001    $0009    $0011    $0019   | ...
Line 2     | $0002    $000A    $0012    $001A   | ...
Line 3     | $0003    $000B    $0013    $001B   | ...
Line 4     | $0004    $000C    $0014    $001C   | ...
Line 5     | $0005    $000D    $0015    $001D   | ...
Line 6     | $0006    $000E    $0016    $001E   | ...
Line 7     | $0007    $000F    $0017    $001F   | ...
           ----------------------------------------
Line 8     | $0100    $0108    $0110    $0118   | ...
Line 9     | $0101    $0109    $0111    $0119   | ...
Line 10    | $0102    $010A    $0112    $011A   | ...
Line 11    | $0103    $010B    $0113    $011B   | ...
              ...      ...      ...      ...      ...
```

Figure 29.5: Pattern table layout of monochrome 1bpp mode

To draw a pixel, we have to first compute the address in the pattern table. This depends on the X and Y positions:

```
word a = (x/8)*16 | ((y&63)/8)*(16*32) | (y&7);
```

If the pixel is in the second or fourth section, we have to use palette 1 instead of palette 0. This is easy — we just use the second eight bits of the tile:

```
if (y & 64) a |= 8;
```

If the pixel is in the third or fourth section, we have to use the second pattern table:

```
if (y & 128) a |= 0x1000;
```

Since we're updating a single pixel, we have to read the byte from VRAM first. This limits how fast we can draw pixels when the screen is active:

```
vram_adr(a);
vram_read(&b, 1);
```

If `color` is non-zero, we set the pixel, otherwise we clear it:

```
if (color) {
  b |= 128 >> (x&7); // set pixel
} else {
  b &= ~(128 >> (x&7)); // clear pixel
}
```

29. CHR RAM

Finally, we write the new byte back to video RAM at the same address:

```
vram_adr(a);
vram_put(b);
```

There aren't a whole lot of applications for this frame buffer method, but it's a neat trick. When the PPU is active, we can only draw one pixel per frame — this is because we read from video RAM for each pixel.

29.2 Other CHR RAM Applications

- We can apply *compression* to the pattern tables in CHR ROM, saving space.
- We can upload new tiles to a pattern table during a game.
- We can render graphics that don't align to the tile grid; for example, proportional fonts and geometric shapes, or objects that are stacked on top of each other.
- We can animate the background by redrawing the tiles — this enables tricks like *parallax scrolling*, where the background scrolls slower than the foreground, creating a 3D effect.
- We can even animate sprites — one popular game redraws the tiles for the player character every frame.
- If you were really clever, you might be able to implement *wireframe graphics* with *double buffering* using the monochrome frame buffer described above, hiding one palette while displaying another.

30

Bank Switching

> Open the example on 8bitworkshop.com: From the **Platforms** menu, select **Game Consoles » NES**, then select the **Bank Switching** project from the Project Selector dropdown.

The Bank Switching example in the 8bitworkshop IDE demonstrates how to use *bank switching* in C. Bank switching allows us to use more than the 32 KB of PRG ROM mapped to the CPU, switching code and data banks in and out during runtime.

This demo uses the *MMC3* mapper. It can support up to 512 KB of *PRG ROM*. These are split into 8 KB banks. The last two banks are fixed at addresses $C000-$FFFF.

We've got some leeway in figuring out what to put in each PRG ROM bank. The 6502 expects six bytes of *CPU vectors* at $FFFA-$FFFF, so those have to go in the $E000-$FFFF fixed bank. We also put C library code there so that it is available no matter which switchable banks are selected. In the other fixed bank at $C000-$DFFF, we put read-only (constant) data and the startup code.

We can add other code to those banks, at least until they fill up. Our configuration will support a total of eight PRG ROM banks.

30. Bank Switching

They'll be named CODE0 through CODE6, and the last one is just named CODE (the default bank).

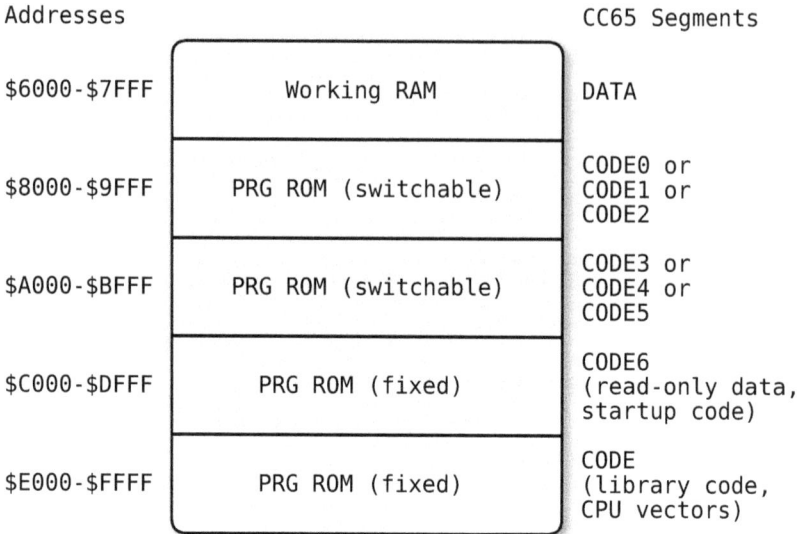

Figure 30.1: MMC3 mapper memory layout

To use the MMC3 mapper, we have to first tell the linker which values to put into the *iNES header*. Just like in Chapter 29, we use preprocessor defines to tell the IDE which parameters to pass to the linker:

```
// bank switching configuration
#define NES_MAPPER 4         // Mapper 4 (MMC3)
#define NES_PRG_BANKS 4      // # of 16KB PRG banks
#define NES_CHR_BANKS 8      // # of 8KB CHR banks
```

By default, constant (read-only) data structures are placed in the CODE *segment*. We have more than one PRG ROM segment, and need a way to select different ones.

We can use a special **#pragma** directive, which gives instructions to the compiler outside of the C standard.

The `rodata-name` pragma changes the current read-only segment in which future *const* declarations will be stored, for example:

```
#pragma rodata-name("CODE0")
const unsigned char TEXT0[]={"Bank 0 @ 8000"};
#pragma rodata-name("CODE1")
const unsigned char TEXT1[]={"Bank 1 @ 8000"};
#pragma rodata-name("CODE5")
const unsigned char TEXT5[]={"Bank 5 @ A000"};
#pragma rodata-name("CODE6")
const unsigned char TEXT6[]={"Bank 6 @ C000"};
```

For C functions, we use the `code-name` pragma. For example, this puts functions below the pragma into the CODE1 segment:

```
#pragma code-name("CODE1")
```

30.1 MMC3 Registers

The MMC3 mapper is controlled by eight registers, arranged in four pairs.

Hex Addr	Name	Bits Used 76543210	Description
$8000	MMC3_BANK_SEL	CPM..RRR	Bank select/mode
$8001	MMC3_BANK_DATA	DDDDDDDD	Bank data
$A000	MMC3_MIRRORING	.......M	0=vertical, 0x80=horizontal
$A001	MMC3_PRG_RAM	RW......	Write-protect PRG RAM (during power off)
$C000	MMC3_IRQ_LATCH	DDDDDDDD	IRQ counter reload value
$C001	MMC3_IRQ_RELOAD	strobe	Reload IRQ counter at next scanline
$E000	MMC3_IRQ_DISABLE	strobe	Disable interrupts
$E001	MMC3_IRQ_ENABLE	strobe	Enable interrupts

Table 30.1: MMC3 Registers

Our *NESLib* library doesn't have explicit support for the MMC3 mapper, but we can build it ourselves. The *peekpoke.h* include

30. Bank Switching

file includes simple macros for *peeking* (reading memory at an arbitrary address) and *poking* (writing memory at an arbitrary address):

```
#include <peekpoke.h>
```

We'll use these peek/poke macros to develop our own macros that manipulate MMC3 registers.

```
#define MMC_MODE 0x00

#define MMC3_SET_REG(r,n)\
POKE(0x8000, MMC_MODE|(r));\
POKE(0x8001, (n));
```

We can now develop macros that switch the PRG ROM banks:

```
#define MMC3_PRG_8000(n) MMC3_SET_REG(6,n)
#define MMC3_PRG_A000(n) MMC3_SET_REG(7,n)
```

Before calling a function or accessing data, you'd need to map the appropriate bank to the correct address region. For example, we have a **draw_text()** function which we've placed in the CODE1 segment:

```
#pragma code-name("CODE1")
void draw_text(word addr, const char* text) {
  vram_adr(addr);
  vram_write(text, strlen(text));
}
```

Before we call this function, we have to select it into address space. We see in Figure 30.1 that the CODE1 segment maps to the $8000-$9FFF region, so we use the MMC3_PRG_8000 macro:

```
  MMC3_PRG_8000(1); // select bank 1
  draw_text(NTADR_A(2,3), TEXT1);
```

If you have a function in a switchable bank that reads data from a different switchable bank, you must switch in both banks before calling the function. For example:

```
  MMC3_PRG_8000(1); // select bank 1 @ $8000
  MMC3_PRG_A000(5); // select bank 5 @ $A000
  draw_text(NTADR_A(2,4), TEXT5);
```

You could easily define a *macro* that does the same thing:

```
#define DRAW_TEXT(addr,text,textbank)\
  MMC3_PRG_8000(1);\
  MMC3_PRG_A000(textbank);\
  draw_text(addr,text)
```

There's nothing stopping you from mapping a bank in the wrong location, for example selecting bank 5 into the $8000 region. The C linker only maps a symbol to a single address, so it'd still assume all CODE5 objects are in the $A000 region. You'd have to do some manual pointer-wrangling if you wanted to do this.

30.2 CHR ROM Switching and Other Features

MMC3 also supports *CHR ROM* bank switching. One pattern table is split into two 2 KB banks (128 tiles each) and the other pattern table is split into four 1 KB banks (64 tiles each). Either pattern table can be used for sprites or background or both, depending on how the PPU_CTRL register is configured.

Here are the macros that switch CHR ROM banks:

```
#define MMC3_CHR_0000(n) MMC3_SET_REG(0,n)
#define MMC3_CHR_0800(n) MMC3_SET_REG(1,n)
#define MMC3_CHR_1000(n) MMC3_SET_REG(2,n)
#define MMC3_CHR_1400(n) MMC3_SET_REG(3,n)
#define MMC3_CHR_1800(n) MMC3_SET_REG(4,n)
#define MMC3_CHR_1C00(n) MMC3_SET_REG(5,n)
```

We can also switch between horizontal and vertical mirroring:

```
#define MMC3_MIRROR(n) POKE(0xa000, (n))
```

The MMC3 mapper also supports 8 KB of PRG RAM, which is mapped to $6000-$7FFF. Our configuration will put all non-readonly variables there by default.

MMC3 also supports IRQs for scanline counting, which we'll discuss in the next chapter.

31

IRQs

We know that the PPU sends an *NMI* (*non-maskable interrupt*) signal to the CPU when the vertical blank period starts, at the end of a video frame.

The 6502 handles another kind of interrupt — *IRQ* (*interrupt request*). These can be generated by the APU, but we're going to focus on IRQs generated by the *MMC3* mapper.

31.1 MMC3 Interrupts

Sometimes it's useful to be able to count scanlines; for example, to split the screen at a certain scanline. We covered the *sprite zero* trick in Chapter 15, which requires that the CPU spin in a busy loop waiting for the sprite zero flag, wasting CPU time.

The MMC3 mapper can count scanlines, and generate an IRQ when a certain number of scanlines have been counted. This frees the CPU to run game logic, and the IRQ service routine will run at the appropriate scanline to implement PPU changes.

The MMC3 has an internal counter, and a *reload value* which can be set via register. The internal counter is decremented at the end of each scanline. When it hits zero, it is reloaded with the reload value, and an IRQ is generated.

31. IRQs

> Open the example on 8bitworkshop.com: From the **Platforms** menu, select **Game Consoles » NES**, then select the **IRQ Scanline Counter** project from the Project Selector dropdown.

Some of the MMC3 registers activate when written to, but they don't care what value is written. We define a new STROBE macro that does this efficiently using *inline assembly*. It just stores whatever is in the A register to a specific address, given by a macro parameter:

```
// "strobe" means "write any value"
#define STROBE(addr) __asm__ ("sta %w", addr)
```

We'll define macros for the MMC3 IRQ registers using STROBE and POKE:

```
#define MMC3_IRQ_SET_VALUE(n)  POKE(0xc000, (n));
#define MMC3_IRQ_RELOAD()      STROBE(0xc001)
#define MMC3_IRQ_DISABLE()     STROBE(0xe000)
#define MMC3_IRQ_ENABLE()      STROBE(0xe001)
```

We want to generate an IRQ every eight scanlines. So we set the IRQ latch value to 7 — it'll count down to zero, then reset.

```
MMC3_IRQ_SET_VALUE(7);
MMC3_IRQ_RELOAD();
MMC3_IRQ_ENABLE();
```

We also have to clear the 6502's *interrupt flag*, which allows it to handle IRQs:

```
__asm__ ("cli"); // enable IRQ
```

Whenever a NMI or IRQ is triggered, NESLib redirects to a *callback* function. We can define our own callback function with **nmi_set_callback()**:

```
nmi_set_callback(irq_nmi_callback);    // set callback func.
```

How do we distinguish between NMI and IRQ interrupts? The IRQ interrupt handler sets the high bit of the A register. We can test it using the built-in __A__ variable:

```c
void __fastcall__ irq_nmi_callback(void) {
  // check high bit of A to see if this is an IRQ
  if (__A__ & 0x80) {
    // it's an IRQ from the MMC3 mapper
    // change PPU scroll registers
    // acknowledge IRQ
  } else {
    // it's a normal NMI
    // reload IRQ counter
  }
}
```

(It would probably be more elegant to add a parameter to the callback function, but this would break existing code that doesn't use IRQs, and we're lazy.)

We won't receive any more IRQs unless we acknowledge the one we just received. We do this by clearing and immediately resetting the IRQ enable flag:

```
MMC3_IRQ_DISABLE();
MMC3_IRQ_ENABLE();
```

31.2 Caveats

The most common use for scanline IRQs is to split the screen without using much CPU time. You can split the screen an arbitrary number of times, as this demo does. You could theoretically generate an IRQ once per scanline, but the IRQ overhead would eat up the majority of CPU time.

Scanline IRQs can also be used as a sort of timer. You could have an IRQ trigger near the end of the visible screen, setting a flag that tells your code to finish whatever it's doing. Unfortunately, this cannot be done during vertical blank, since the scanline counter won't be counting.

The NES was not really designed for scanline counting, so the MMC3 mapper uses a clever hack — it looks for certain patterns on the PPU's address bus when it accesses memory. During each scanline, the PPU fetches nametable and background tile patterns, then fetches sprite patterns. If the background uses

31. IRQs

the first pattern table ($0000-$0FFF) and the sprites use the second pattern table ($1000-$1FFF), the A12 address line will wiggle exactly once per scanline, right after the visible data.

At least, that's the theory. There's a situation where this scheme doesn't work, however. If the PPU is set to use 8x16 sprites, it could read sprite patterns anywhere in pattern memory. This could cause the A12 line to oscillate more than once, depending on which sprites are shown on a given scanline.

32

Sprite Starfield

If our game is set in outer space, we might like to see a starfield slowly scrolling behind our sprites.

We could draw the stars into the nametable, and use the scroll registers to move them. This would only work if the entire background contains stars, unless we use a *screen split* technique.

Another method that works when using *CHR RAM* is to animate the pattern table. Let's say we reserve 16 tiles for stars. Only one of those tiles contains a single-pixel star; the rest are blank. Each frame, we erase the current pixel in the pattern table and draw a new pixel directly above or below it. This requires only two PPU writes per frame.

 Open the example on 8bitworkshop.com: From the **Platforms** menu, select **Game Consoles » NES**, then select the **Solarian Game** project from the Project Selector dropdown.

Our solution for the *Solarian* game is to use a single sprite per star. The drawback is that there are only 64 sprite slots in OAM and eight sprites per line, so we can only do this because our game doesn't use many sprites. (It animates the background tiles, as we learned in Chapter 29.)

32. Sprite Starfield

We'll use 32 sprites, spacing them eight lines apart. This ensures that we only have one star sprite per scanline, and the other seven slots are available.

We want the star sprites to take up sprite slots 0-31. The rest of the game's sprites will take up sprite slots 32-63. This allows us to use **oam_hide_rest()** without erasing any stars.

We initialize our stars randomly, directly into the OAM buffer:

```
void init_stars() {
  byte oamid = 0; // 32 slots = 128 bytes
  byte i;
  for (i=0; i<32; i++) {
    oamid = oam_spr(rand(), i*8, 103+(i&3), 0|OAM_BEHIND,
      oamid);
  }
}
```

The only parameter that changes frame-to-frame is the Y coordinate. We can use this fact to optimize this function. Instead of calling **oam_spr()**, we can just set the Y coordinate directly in the OAM buffer. When we want to move the sprites, we modify the Y coordinate directly via the OAMBUF array:

```
void draw_stars_c() {
  byte i;
  for (i=0; i<32; i++) {
    ++OAMBUF[i].y;
  }
}
```

OAMBUF is defined in **neslib.h**. It's a 64-element array of OAMSprite structs, starting at address $200:

```
typedef struct OAMSprite {
  byte y;      // Y coordinate
  byte name;   // tile index in name table
  byte attr;   // attribute flags
  byte x;      // X coordinate
} OAMSprite;

#define OAMBUF            ((OAMSprite*) 0x200)
```

In fact, we don't really need to use **oam_spr()**, because we can set up sprites through this array. But the **cc65** compiler does not manipulate C structs very efficiently. Using C to move 32 sprites every frame might take too long.

We can make the **draw_stars()** function a little faster by using *inline assembly*. This allows us to inject assembly statements right inside of a C function, using the **asm** keyword.

Instead of accessing the OAM buffer via array of structs, we just increment every fourth byte:

```
void draw_stars() {
  asm("ldy #0");        // start with Y = 0
  asm("clc");           // clear carry for addition
  asm("@1: lda $200,y");// read from OAM buffer
  asm("adc #1");        // increment
  asm("sta $200,y");    // write to OAM buffer
  asm("iny");           // increment Y by 4
  asm("iny");
  asm("iny");
  asm("iny");
  asm("bpl @1");        // branch while < 128
}
```

We'll dig deeper into the 6502 and programming the NES in assembly language next, in Chapter 33.

 How could you give stars varying speeds? How would you make them blink?

33

The 6502 CPU

The CPU chip in the NES is not technically a MOS Technology 6502, but a *Ricoh 2A03*. This is one of two custom chips in the NES. It contains a mostly-complete 6502 core, omitting support for *BCD* (decimal) mode. The chip package also contains the *APU* (sound generator) and handles joystick polling.

> Note: If you're already familiar with the 6502, or if you've read my previous book *Making Games for the Atari 2600*, you can safely skip to the next chapter.

33.1 The CPU and the Bus

Think of the CPU as an intricate timepiece. An electronic spring unwinds and an internal clock ticks millions of times per second. On every tick, electrons turn tiny gears, and the

Figure 33.1: Ricoh RP2A03 (CC BY-SA 3.0, by BABAX)

33. THE 6502 CPU

CPU comes to rest in a different state. Each tick is called a *clock cycle*, or *CPU clock*.

All the CPU does is execute instructions, one after another. It fetches an instruction (reads it from memory), decodes it (figures out what to do), and then executes it (does some things in a prescribed order). Each instruction may take several clock cycles to execute, each clock cycle performing a specific step. The CPU then figures out which instruction to grab next, and repeats the process.

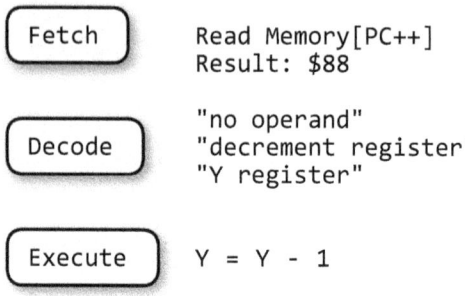

Figure 33.2: CPU Cycle

During each clock cycle, the CPU can read from or write to the bus. The bus is a set of "lanes" where each lane can hold a single bit at a time. In an 8-bit processor, the *data bus* is eight bits (one byte) wide.

Devices like memory, sound synths, and video generators are attached to the bus, and receive read and write signals. The CPU doesn't know which devices are connected to the bus — all it knows is that it either receives eight bits back from a read, or sends eight bits back out into the world during a write.

As bytes are read into the CPU, they are temporarily stored in *registers*, where they can be manipulated further or written back out into the world.

Besides the 8-bit data bus, our CPU has a 16-bit *address bus*. The address bus describes "where" and the data bus describes "what." Since the address bus is 16 bits wide, this gives us 65,536 possible addresses that we can target, each address representing a single byte.

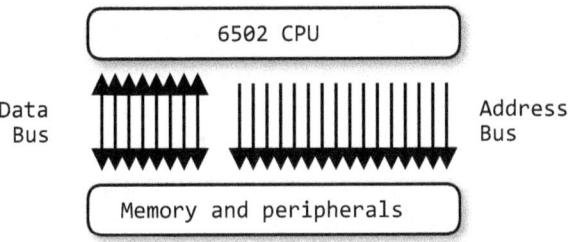

Figure 33.3: 6502 data and address buses

33.2 CPU Instructions

Let's look at what happens when the CPU executes this example instruction, LDA (LoaD A):

lda $1234

The CPU will set the pins on the address bus to the binary encoding for $1234, set the read/write pin to "read," and wait for a response on the data bus. Devices on the bus look at the address $1234 and determine whether the message is for them — by design, only one device should respond. The CPU then reads the value from the data bus and puts it into the A register.

Let's say we are executing the STA instruction (STore A):

sta $1234

The CPU will set the address bus to $1234 and the data bus to whatever is in the A register, then set the read/write pin to "write." Again, the bus devices look at the address bus and the write signal and decide if they should listen or ignore it. Let's say a memory chip responds — the memory chip would read the 8-bit value off the data bus and store it in the memory cell corresponding to address $1234. The CPU does not get a response from a write; it just assumes everything worked out fine.

You'll note that both of these instructions operate on the A register. The 6502 has three general-purpose registers: A, X, and Y. These are all 8-bit variables that you can manipulate at will. You'll often have to use the registers as temporary storage,

33. The 6502 CPU

for instance: Load a constant value into A, then store A to a given address.

You'll notice that the CPU instructions have a three-letter format. This is called a *mnemonic*, and it's part of the human-readable language used by the CPU, called *assembly* language. The CPU doesn't understand this, but it understands a compact code called *machine code*. A program called an *assembler* takes the human-readable assembly code and produces machine code.

Let's take another example instruction:

    lda $1234   ; ad 34 12

The machine code for this instruction is three bytes, $ad, $34, and $12. $ad is the *opcode* which identifies the instruction and addressing mode. $34 and $12 are part of the *operand*, which in this case is a 16-bit number spanning two bytes. You'll note that the $34 is first and the $12 is second — this is because the 6502 is a *little-endian* processor, expecting the least-significant parts of multibyte quantities first.

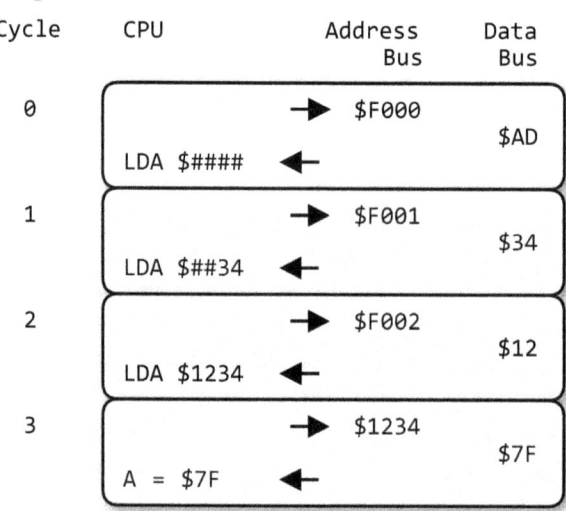

Figure 33.4: LDA Cycle

33.3 Writing Loops

Now we're ready to write a program. Typically, we'd start with the classic example that prints "Hello, World" on the display, but we don't have a display yet! So we'll start with something simpler: a loop that counts from 100 (decimal) down to zero.

```
        ldy #100      ; Y = 100
Loop:   dey           ; subtract 1 from Y
        bne Loop      ; repeat until Y == 0
```

Here we have three instructions and one *label* named Loop. A label associates a name with a location in your code. You can reference the label anywhere else in your code, and the assembler will ensure it refers to the correct address in memory.

> Each 6502 assembler *dialect* has its own syntax. Here, comments start with a ";" and go until the end of the line. Labels are flush against the left margin and followed by a colon and can be placed on their own line or on the same line as an instruction (although for some assemblers, like **DASM**, the colon is optional).

The first instruction LDY (LoaD Y) loads the Y register with a constant value, 100. Constants start with a "#" and tell the assembler to use the value directly, not as a memory-load or memory-store instruction.

The next instruction DEY (DEcrement Y) subtracts 1 from the Y register. It also sets the Zero (Z) flag in the CPU, which is an internal bit that is set to 1 if the result of an instruction is zero. We use these *flags* to test for conditions in the code.

The final instruction BNE (Branch Not Equal) is a branch instruction, which means the next instruction may be one of two choices. BNE transfers control to its target label if the Z flag is unset, and will fall through to the next instruction if it is set. In our case, since DEY just set the Z flag, the branch will be taken

33. The 6502 CPU

until the Y register decreases to zero, and so the loop will repeat 100 times.

Let's make a loop that uses the different *addressing modes* of the 6502. These allow you to target areas of memory beyond a single constant location, by adding another register to an address. For example, this demonstrates the *absolute indexed* addressing mode with the STA instruction:

```
        lda #0          ; A <- 0
        ldy #$7F        ; Y <- 127
Loop:   sta $100,y      ; store A in [$100+y]
        dey             ; decrement Y, set flags
        bne Loop        ; repeat until Y == 0
```

This loop makes use of two registers: A and Y. A is initialized to zero and Y counts down from $7F (127) to zero. The STA (STore Accumulator) instruction stores A to an address at every loop iteration. We use the addressing mode "absolute,indexed" here, which means we compute the destination address by adding a register (Y in this case) to a constant ($100 in this case). Since Y counts from $7F down to zero, we'll store A (which we set to 0) to addresses $17F to $100 in decreasing order.

In 6502 parlance, the *absolute indexed* mode means "add an 8-bit value (Y register in this case) to a 16-bit constant." There is another mode, *zero page* mode, which operates only on 8-bit values. Zero page refers to the memory locations $00-$FF which get special treatment. Instructions that use zero-page addressing modes are smaller and run faster, so it's common to put often-used variables in this region.

There are restrictions to these modes, and all combinations do not have a corresponding encoding. For example, only X and Y can be used as indices, the A register cannot be used as an index. Also, Y can only be used as a zero-page index with the LDX and STX instructions — otherwise it is expanded to an absolute index. Your assembler will throw an error if you try to use an invalid addressing mode.

Our last loop has a problem, though. We used the BNE instruction to repeat the loop until Y is zero. But since the store happens before we decrement Y, we don't store anything when Y is zero! To fix this, we just change the loop so that the DEY happens before the STA, and add 1 to the starting Y value:

```
        lda #0
        ldy #$80        ; Y <- 128
Loop:   dey             ; set flags
        sta $100,y      ; does not modify flags
        bne Loop        ; repeat while Y != 0
```

Since STA does not modify any flags, we can DEY first (which does modify flags) and then exit the loop when Y==0 rather than Y<0.

We could also count upwards from zero using the CPY (ComPare Y) instruction:

```
        lda #0
        tay             ; Y <- 0
Loop:   sta $100,y
        iny
        cpy #$80        ; set flags as if (Y - 128)
        bne Loop        ; branch until Y == 128
```

The CPY instruction performs a comparison: It subtracts the operand from the Y register and sets flags, but discards the result. So, in this example, if Y is $80, (Y-$80) will be zero and the Zero flag will be set. There is a compare instruction for each of the three registers:

CMP	Compare A to memory location
CPX	Compare X to memory location
CPY	Compare Y to memory location

33.4 Condition Flags and Branching

We've covered the Z (Zero) flag already, but there are others. Table 33.4 lists the condition flags you'll be using most often.

33. THE 6502 CPU

Flag	Name	Description
Z	Zero	Set when the result is zero.
N	Negative/Sign	Set when the result is negative (high bit set).
C	Carry	Set when an arithmetic operation wraps and carries the high bit.
V	Overflow	Set when an arithmetic operation overflows; i.e. if the sign of the result changes due to overflow.

Table 33.1: Condition Flags

A lot of instructions just set the Zero and Negative flags, which makes it easy to test for zero values or to test the high bit. The Carry flag is set by compare, add, subtract, and shift operations.

The Overflow bit is less commonly used than the Carry bit, but it's worth explaining the difference between *wrapping* and *overflow*. When we say a value wraps, we mean that an operation exceeds the boundaries of its byte and the result is truncated. So if you add $01 to $FF, you'll wrap around to $00.

The *overflow* flag is set when the result of a addition or subtraction changes its sign — for example, $40 + $40 = $80 — which overflows because $80 is a negative number in two's complement representation. If you're using unsigned numbers, you can generally ignore this flag.

Mnem.	Description	Flag Test	Condition
BNE	Not Equal	Zero clear	A != B
BEQ	Equal	Zero set	A == B
BCC	Carry Clear	Carry clear	A < B (unsigned)
BCS	Carry Set	Carry set	A ≥ B (unsigned)
BMI	Minus	Negative set	A < B (signed)
BPL	Plus	Negative clear	A ≥ B (signed)
BVC		Overflow clear	no signed overflow
BVS		Overflow set	signed overflow
JMP	Jump	—	always taken

Table 33.2: Branch Instructions

The JMP instruction doesn't test any flags but just moves the PC directly to the target. The branch instructions can only modify the PC by -128 to +127 bytes, so for longer distances, you'll need JMP.

It's good to memorize the BCC (less than) and BCS (greater than or equal) instructions, since these are used often. Also note that the BPL and BMI instructions are the same for signed quantities, so we could use them to stop when a value goes negative, like this:

```
       lda #0        ; A <- 0
       ldy #$7F      ; Y <- 127
Loop:  sta $100,y    ; store A in [$100+y]
       dey           ; decrement Y, set flags
       bpl Loop      ; repeat until signed(Y) < 0
```

Note that this technique would not work if we started with Y = $81 or higher, because the first DEY would result in a negative number, exiting the loop on the first iteration!

33.5 Addition and Subtraction

We've covered DEY, but there is an entire group of instructions that increment (add one) or decrement (subtract one):

DEC	-1 from memory location
DEX	-1 from X register
DEY	-1 from Y register
INC	+1 to memory location
INX	+1 to X register
INY	+1 to Y register

There's no INC or DEC for the A register, but you can add or subtract the A register to/from another memory location or constant using these instructions:

ADC	Add memory location to A
SBC	Subtract memory location from A
CLC	Clear carry flag
SEC	Set carry flag

An example of addition:

```
lda $81  ; load memory location $81 -> A
clc      ; clear carry flag
adc #10  ; add 10 to A
sta $82  ; store A -> memory location $82
```

Note the CLC (Clear Carry Flag) instruction. The ADC instruction adds the Carry flag to the result (0 or 1) so usually it must be cleared before addition. For subtraction, it must be set first using SEC (Set Carry Flag):

```
lda $81  ; load memory location $81 -> A
sec      ; set carry flag
sbc #10  ; subtract 10 from A
sta $82  ; store A -> memory location $82
```

The increment/decrement instructions modify the Negative and Zero flags, while the addition/subtraction additionally modify the Carry flag. The compare instructions (CMP/CPX/CPY) perform a subtraction, throwing away the result but keeping the flags.

33.6 The Stack

In computing terminology, a *stack* is a list of values that can grow and shrink. You grow the stack by *pushing* a value on top, and shrink by *pulling* a value off the top (note that *pull* is referred to as *pop* on most other processors; but 6502 instructions use *pull*).

On the 6502, the stack is stored at memory locations $0100-$01FF. The S (*stack pointer*) register stores the lower eight bits of this register — the top eight bits are hard-coded to $01. This register is usually initialized to $FF. These instructions modify the stack:

PHA		Push A register to stack
PLA		Pull A register from stack
PHP		Push flags register to stack
PLP		Pull flags register from stack
JSR		Jump to Subroutine
RTS		Return from Subroutine
RTI		Return from Interrupt

The PHA instruction pushes the A register to the stack, storing it to the memory location pointed to by S. It then decrements S by 1. We say the stack "grows upward" because the stack pointer decreases as new values are added.

You can retrieve the top value on the stack with the PLA instruction. It first increments S by 1, then reads the location pointed to by S into A.

Another important instruction that uses the stack is JSR. It pushes the Program Counter to the stack, then transfers control to another location, just like a JMP. When the RTS instruction is encountered, the CPU pulls the top address off of the stack and transfers control there. RTI is used to return from an *interrupt*, which we'll discuss later.

33.7 Logical Operations

AND	A&B	Set bit if A and B are set.
ORA	A|B	Set bit if A or B (or both) are set.
EOR	A^B	Set bit if either A or B are set, but not both (exclusive-or).
BIT	A&B	Same as AND, but just set flags and throw away the result.

33. The 6502 CPU

The "logical" instructions combine the bits of the A register and the operand, performing a bit (logic) operation on each bit.

33.8 Shift Operations

ASL	Shift Left	Shift left 1 bit, bit 7 → Carry
LSR	Shift Right	Shift right 1 bit, bit 0 → Carry
ROL	Rotate Left	Same as ASL except Carry → bit 0
ROR	Rotate Right	Same as LSR except Carry → bit 7

There is also the family of "shift" operations that move bits left and right by one position within a byte. The bit that is shifted off the edge of the byte (i.e., the high bit for shift left, and the low bit for shift right) gets put into the Carry flag.

The "rotate" operations are similar, but they also shift the previous Carry flag into the other end of the byte. So for rotate left, the Carry flag is copied into the rightmost (low) bit. For rotate right, it's copied into the leftmost (high) bit.

The A register is implied, as with the arithmetic and logical instructions. Here's an example of ASL (shift left):

```
lda #$83      ; A = $83
asl           ; shift A left by 1
```

And here's its result (C means that the carry flag is set):

```
              $83  10000011
ASL    ->     $06  00000110   C
```

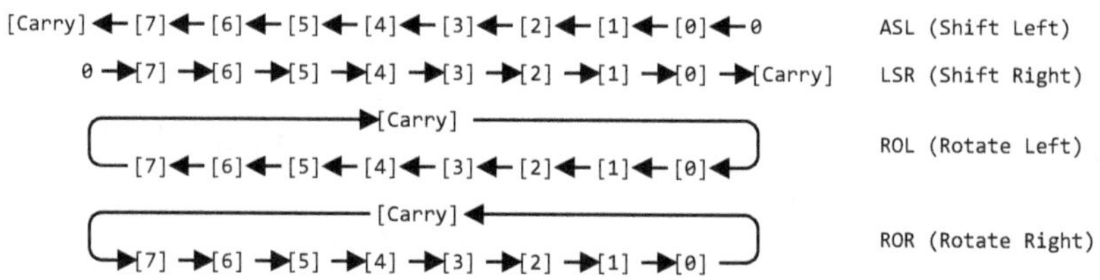

[Carry] ← [7] ← [6] ← [5] ← [4] ← [3] ← [2] ← [1] ← [0] ← 0   ASL (Shift Left)
0 → [7] → [6] → [5] → [4] → [3] → [2] → [1] → [0] → [Carry]   LSR (Shift Right)
→ [Carry] → [7] ← [6] ← [5] ← [4] ← [3] ← [2] ← [1] ← [0] ←   ROL (Rotate Left)
[Carry] ← [7] → [6] → [5] → [4] → [3] → [2] → [1] → [0] →   ROR (Rotate Right)

Figure 33.5: Shift and rotate bit flow

Another example, this time of ROR (rotate right):

```
lda #$03
sec        ; set carry flag
ror        ; rotate right
ror        ; rotate right
ror        ; rotate right
```

Note that we use SEC to set the carry first. Here's the result:

		$03	00000011	C
ROR	->	$81	10000001	C
ROR	->	$81	11000000	C
ROR	->	$81	11100000	

Note that if you ROL or ROR nine times in succession, you'd return to the original byte.

The 6502 lacks multiplication and division instructions, but bit shifts can multiply and divide by powers of two. Each left shift multiplies by 2, and each right shift divides by 2 (rounding down for unsigned numbers).

33.9 Indirect Addressing

We've already talked about the *absolute indexed* and *zero page indexed* addressing modes in this chapter. These allow reading of memory at an offset from a fixed address. But what if the address is not fixed? This is where *indirect addressing* modes are useful.

The *indirect indexed* mode is equivalent to a *array lookup* in C, albeit one limited to an 8 bit index:

```
ldy #5
lda ($80),y     ; indirect indexed
```

The expression ($80),y is an *indirect indexed* addressing mode. Here, we are instructing the CPU to look up the 16-bit value at $80 and $81 (low byte and high byte), convert it to an address, then add the Y register to it. That will be the final address used for the instruction, which in this case is the address that the lda instruction reads from memory.

```
ldy #4          ; Y <- 4
lda ($80),y     ; address is {mem[$80],mem[$81]} + Y
```

The other indirect mode is called *indexed indirect*, where the addition takes place before the address lookup:

```
ldx #4          ; X <- 4
lda ($80,x)     ; address is {mem[$80+X],mem[$81+X]}
```

If X is 4, then the CPU looks up the 16-bit pointer at address $84 and $85, and then loads the value contained at the pointer's address.

33.10 Whew!

That was a long overview. Don't feel compelled to memorize everything up-front. We're about to get into NES programming and we'll go over many examples of 6502 code.

34

Hello NES Assembly

We're going to jump right in and write a simple program for the NES in 6502 assembler. Our first program won't do much — it'll just initialize the PPU and set the screen background color.

Proper initialization of the NES requires a number of steps. We have to wait for the PPU to "warm up" and reset it to a known state. This is to ensure the code runs properly on actual hardware, and that the reset button works the same as a cold power-up.

Open the example on 8bitworkshop.com: From the **Platforms** menu, select **Game Consoles » NES**, then select the **Initialization (ASM)** project from the Project Selector dropdown.

34.1 Equates

There's a lot of memory locations in the NES to memorize. No one likes keeping a bunch of weird numbers in their head, so the assembler helps you track all of these memory locations. The **equ** (*equate*) directive lets you map a friendly name to a constant or an address.

For example, to define the PPU_CTRL register, which maps to address $2000, we'd issue the following EQU statement ("=" does the same thing):

```
PPU_CTRL      equ $2000      ; define a constant
PPU_CTRL      =   $2000      ; same thing
```

Equates aren't just limited to memory locations. Say we wanted to define the number of starting lives as a constant:

```
StartLives    equ   5        ; start with five lives
```

Using an equate is easy: just type its name. You may be tempted to do something like this:

```
lda StartLives               ; load the number 5 (WRONG!!!!)
sta LivesLeft                ; store in memory
```

But this would load the value read from address 5, not the number 5! The assembler can't distinguish between a constant and an address. So we add a "#" to let the assembler know that StartLives should be treated as a constant:

```
lda #StartLives              ; load the number 5 with "#"
sta LivesLeft                ; store in memory
```

The IDE has several *include files* which provide useful constants and memory locations for the NES.

34.2 Includes and Segments

The assembler we'll use is called **DASM**, which is the same one used in our *Making Games for the Atari 2600* book. It uses a different assembly language dialect than the .s files output by the cc65 compiler and assembled by the ca65 assembler.

First, we use the **include** directive to import an include file named **nesdefs.dasm**, which contains some useful NES-specific symbols and definitions. It also issues a **processor 6502** directive, which tells the assembler we're using 6502 instructions, so we need to include it before writing any code:

```
include "nesdefs.dasm"
```

We will also want to define a *segment* for *zero page* variables:

```
seg.u ZEROPAGE
org $0
```

This is a special region of RAM ranging from address $00 to address $FF where we will place our frequently-used variables. Segments aren't strictly necessary in *DASM*, since there's no *link* step, but they can be useful for organization.

The **seg.u** directive defines an *uninitialized segment* (i.e., no code goes here, just variables) called Zeropage. The **org** directive sets the address of the first variable to 0. We don't have any variables in this example, so we'll leave it empty for now.

34.3 The iNES Header

Now we have to define the *iNES header*, which is a 16-byte structure at the beginning of a ROM file. This is a standard used by all NES emulators to describe the cartridge.

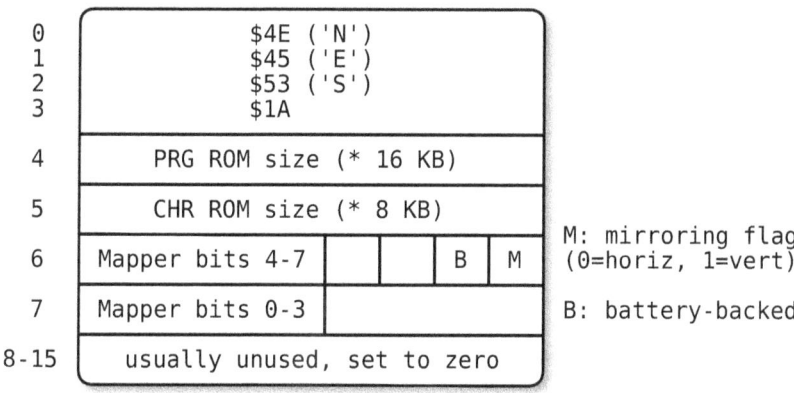

Figure 34.1: iNES Header

The most commonly-used fields are:

Mapper: NES cartridges may contain circuits that expand the range of ROM and RAM space, as well as add additional features not supported by the base platform. These are called *mappers*, and the iNES format defines hundreds of different types. Our

34. Hello NES Assembly

assembler examples use the relatively simple mapper 0, which is also called *NROM*.

PRG ROM Size: We also have to declare how many *PRG ROM* (program) bytes are in the file, in increments of 16 KB. Most of our examples use 32 KB, which is the maximum we can have without *bank switching*.

CHR ROM Size: How many *CHR ROM* banks are in the file, in increments of 8 KB (512 tiles). Most of our examples use a single 8 KB CHR ROM bank. We could also put a zero here if we're using *CHR RAM*.

Mirroring: Lastly, we define the nametable *mirroring* scheme. This setting usually depends on the dominant scroll direction (vertical, horizontal, or omnidirectional) and whether or not a status bar is present. We covered this in Chapter 10.

We can generate an iNES Header in assembly language using the NES_HEADER *macro*:

```
NES_HEADER 0,2,1,0
```

A *macro* is an identifier, traditionally written in all caps. It has a definition, which is just a body of text. When the assembler or compiler sees a macro, it substitutes its definition. A macro can also have parameters, with are also substituted.

The NES_HEADER macro is equivalent to the following:

```
seg Header         ; Header segment
org $7FF0          ; start header at $7FF0
byte $4e,$45,$53,$1a ; header
byte .NES_PRG_BANKS
byte .NES_CHR_BANKS
byte .NES_MIRRORING|(.NES_MAPPER<<4)
byte .NES_MAPPER&$f0
byte 0,0,0,0,0,0,0,0
seg Code           ; Code segment
org $8000          ; start code at $8000
```

The **seg** directive starts a new segment called Header. This segment will contain our 16-byte iNES header. The **org** directive tells the assembler that the segment starts at address $7FF0, 16 bytes before the Code segment. The **byte** directives output the 16 bytes of the header.

Before finishing, the macro begins the Code segment which will contain our PRG ROM code starting at $8000.

34.4 The NES_INIT Macro

We first define the label Start. This is the address that the CPU will start executing when the console is reset. The first thing we do is expand the NES_INIT macro:

```
Start:
        NES_INIT      ; set up stack pointer, turn off PPU
```

NES_INIT, included in **nesdefs.asm**, does a whole bunch of stuff to initialize the CPU and PPU. Let's go through what it does in detail. Here are its first lines:

```
        sei           ; disable IRQs
        cld           ; decimal mode not supported
```

The macro first uses SEI to set the I flag which, in the 6502, disables *interrupt requests* (*IRQs*). Then it does a CLD to clear the D or *decimal flag*.[1]

The next two instructions set up the S register, also known as the *stack pointer*:

```
        ldx #$ff      ; $ff -> X register
        txs           ; X -> stack pointer
```

The stack pointer usually begins at $FF. All stack operations occur in page 1 ($100-$1FF), so our stack will start at $1FF and grow upward — that is, the stack pointer decreases as we push items onto the stack.

---

[1] As we noted in Chapter 23, the 6502 core in the NES has no support for BCD (*binary-coded decimal*) mode.

34. Hello NES Assembly

The macro sets a few other registers, which turns off the PPU's rendering and various sources of interrupts:

```
inx                 ; increment X to 0
stx PPU_MASK        ; disable PPU rendering
stx DMC_FREQ        ; disable DMC interrupts
stx PPU_CTRL        ; disable NMI interrupts
```

This code sets all of these registers to zero. The macro previously set the X register to $FF, so INX wraps it to zero. This saves one byte vs. a LDA #$00.

It's a good idea to read the PPU_STATUS register at startup. This resets the vertical blank flag, the sprite zero flag, and the internal flag that flips between the high and low bytes of PPU_ADDR and PPU_SCROLL:

```
bit PPU_STATUS      ;clear VBL flag
```

Lastly, the macro sets some APU registers to ensure silence:

```
bit APU_CHAN_CTRL   ;ack DMC IRQ bit 7
lda #$40
sta APU_FRAME       ;disable APU Frame IRQ
lda #$0F
sta APU_CHAN_CTRL   ;disable DMC, enable channels
```

And that's the end of the NES_INIT macro.

34.5 Warming up the PPU

One of the goals of the startup sequence is to ensure we wait at least 29,658 cycles for the PPU to "warm up," initializing its internal state. The easiest way is to wait two video frames, each of which takes 27,384 cycles.

First, we call our first subroutine WaitSync, which waits for the PPU to start its next vertical blank period, which would be the next video frame:

```
jsr WaitSync        ; wait for VSYNC
```

34.5. Warming up the PPU

We do this by checking the high bit of the PPU_STATUS register with the BIT instruction, then looping until we see that the bit is set:

```
WaitSync:
        bit PPU_STATUS      ; bit 7 -> N flag
        bpl WaitSync        ; loop while N flag is clear
        rts                 ; high bit is set, return
```

Due to a hardware race condition, this is an unreliable way to wait for vertical blank, as it occasionally misses frames. It's fine for PPU warm-up, but don't use it during a game — use the *NMI* handler instead.

The next thing we should do is clear all of the RAM accessible to the CPU. We'll use the X register to count from 0 to 255. During each loop iteration, we'll write a zero into memory location 0+X, 256+X, 512+X, etc. This will clear all of the built-in CPU-accessible RAM.

This is a subroutine, so we have to be careful not to erase the stack, or the RTS instruction will not know where to return. This is the reason we've added the .skipStack branch.

```
ClearRAM: subroutine
        lda #0              ; 0 -> A
        tax                 ; 0 -> X
.clearRAM
        sta $0,x            ; 0 -> mem[$0+X]
        cpx #$fe            ; last 2 bytes of stack?
        bcs .skipStack      ; don't clear it
        sta $100,x          ; 0 -> mem[$100+X]
.skipStack
        sta $200,x          ; 0 -> mem[$200+X]
        sta $300,x          ; 0 -> mem[$300+X]
        sta $400,x          ; 0 -> mem[$400+X]
        sta $500,x          ; 0 -> mem[$500+X]
        sta $600,x          ; 0 -> mem[$600+X]
        sta $700,x          ; 0 -> mem[$700+X]
        inx                 ; increment X
        bne .clearRAM       ; repeat until X = 0
        rts
```

While we've wasted a number of cycles already, we still need to wait another full frame to ensure that the PPU is fully warmed up.

34. Hello NES Assembly

So we call `WaitSync` again:

```
jsr WaitSync      ; wait for VBLANK again
```

34.6 Setting the Palette Colors

Now that the PPU is warmed up, we want to prove it by setting the background color. First, we set the PPU_ADDR register to $3F00. This is the beginning of the palette area.

The PPU address is 16 bits long, but the PPU_ADDR register is only eight bits wide. This is handled using an invisible flag that flips every time the PPU_ADDR is written. It alternates setting the upper and lower eight bits of the PPU address. So we write to this register twice:

```
lda #$3f          ; $3f -> A register
sta PPU_ADDR      ; write high byte first
lda #$00          ; $00 -> A register
sta PPU_ADDR      ; $3f00 -> PPU address
```

This flag is reset whenever PPU_STATUS is read, which we do at initialization. You could also do this once per frame or more often if you are worried about having an odd number of PPU_ADDR writes.

Now the PPU address should be set to $3F00, the screen color palette entry. We write to the PPU_DATA register to change this entry.

```
lda #$1c          ; $1c = light blue color
sta PPU_DATA      ; $1c -> PPU data
```

We can only effectively write to PPU RAM while the PPU is disabled, or during *vertical blank*. While the PPU is drawing the frame, the PPU address register continuously increments, preventing us from setting a specific location. In this example, the PPU has not yet been activated.

34.7 Enabling Rendering

Now, we can turn on the PPU. We set the PPU_CTRL and PPU_MASK registers to enable video rendering.

```
lda #MASK_BG     ; A = $08
sta PPU_MASK     ; enable rendering
lda #CTRL_NMI    ; A = $80
sta PPU_CTRL     ; enable NMI
```

In the `PPU_MASK` register, we set the `MASK_BG` bit which enables rendering of the background. The PPU will start rendering scanlines, which for now is just a gray background.

We also enable the `CTRL_NMI` bit in the `PPU_CTRL` register, which enables *NMI* interrupts. We'll explain these in the next section.

We don't have anything else to do, so we just go into an endless loop:

```
.endless
        jmp .endless     ; endless loop
```

From this point, the PPU will happily output dark gray frames until the console is reset or switched off.

34.8 CPU Vectors and Interrupts

There's one more thing we need to complete our ROM. The 6502 expects three 16-bit *CPU vectors* at addresses $FFFA-$FFFF. These tell the CPU what address to jump to when a reset or interrupt is triggered:

Name	Addresses	When triggered?
NMI	$FFFA-$FFFB	at VBLANK
RESET	$FFFC-$FFFD	at power on or reset
IRQ/BRK	$FFFE-$FFFF	requested by mapper or APU

At power-up or reset, the 6502 reads a 16-bit address from the reset vector at $FFFC and loads it into the Program Counter.

Similarly, when an interrupt occurs, the CPU uses the *NMI* (*non-maskable interrupt*) and *IRQ* (*interrupt request*) vectors to locate the interrupt routines. When the CPU receives these signals, it pushes the processor flags and Program Counter onto the stack, then transfers control to the address found in these vectors.

34. Hello NES Assembly

The `NES_VECTORS` macro adds the CPU vectors to PRG ROM:

```
NES_VECTORS       ; CPU vectors @ $FFFA-$FFFF
```

This macro uses the **org** directive to skip to the correct ROM location, then uses **.word** to define these vectors.

Let's look at the macro in **nesdefs.dasm**:

```
MAC NES_VECTORS
seg Vectors              ; segment "Vectors"
org $fffa                ; start at address $fffa
.word NMIHandler         ; $fffa vblank nmi
.word Start              ; $fffc reset
.word NMIHandler         ; $fffe irq / brk
ENDM
```

The `reset` vector points to the `Start` label, which initializes the NES and starts the program.

The NMI and IRQ vectors both point to the `NMIHandler` label. This routine runs every video frame before vertical blank. In this example, it does nothing:

```
NMIHandler:
    rti    ; return from interrupt routine
```

It only has one instruction, `RTI` (Return from Interrupt), which exits the interrupt handler and returns the CPU to what it was doing beforehand.

This seems like a lot of effort to display a blank screen! When we use C programming, a lot of the nuts-and-bolts are hidden in libraries — including the entire initialization sequence. But there will still be times when we'll need to manipulate PPU registers directly.

 Can you add code to the NMI handler to change the color of the screen every frame?

35

Drawing Text in Assembly

In the previous chapter, we initialized the PPU and generated a blank screen. Now we're going to put some text on it.

> Open the example on 8bitworkshop.com: From the **Platforms** menu, select **Game Consoles** » **NES**, then select the **Hello World (ASM)** project from the Project Selector dropdown.

35.1 Setting the Palette

First, we've got to set the palette so we can display characters. We'll create a routine called SetPalette that loads colors from a 32-byte lookup table, and sends each one to the PPU. We'll define a label for it:

SetPalette: **subroutine**

The **subroutine** keyword is specific to the *DASM* assembler. It ensures that any local labels (those that begin with ".") are only accessible inside the subroutine.

35. Drawing Text in Assembly

The palette lives at addresses $3F00-$3F1F (32 bytes) in the PPU. So we'll first set the PPU's address to $3F00, the beginning of the palette region. We did this in the previous chapter, but there's a handy *macro* we can use:

```
PPU_SETADDR $3f00       ; set PPU address to $3f00
```

This macro expands to four instructions:

```
lda #$3f                ; A = $3F
sta PPU_ADDR            ; set high byte first
lda #$00                ; A = $00
sta PPU_ADDR            ; set low byte second
```

The PPU address is then set to the beginning of the palette. Now we loop 32 times, loading each byte in turn from PRG ROM, then sending it to the PPU_DATA register.

Each time we write to PPU_DATA, the PPU *increments* (adds one to) the PPU address. This makes it easy to set contiguous bytes without writing to PPU_ADDR. You can also increment the address by 32 bytes per write by setting the CTRL_INC_32 flag in PPU_CTRL.

After setting the PPU address, our SetPalette routine goes into a loop. We use the Y register to count from 0 to 32. Each loop iteration, we load the byte at address (Palette + Y), then we store it to the PPU_DATA register:

```
        ldy #0          ; Y = 0
.loop:
        lda Palette,y   ; lookup byte in ROM
        sta PPU_DATA    ; store byte to PPU data
        iny             ; Y = Y + 1
        cpy #32         ; is Y equal to 32?
        bne .loop       ; not yet, loop
        rts             ; return to caller
```

To call the routine, we use a JSR instruction:

```
        jsr SetPalette  ; set palette colors
```

We need to also define the array that holds all 32 bytes of the palette data. This is defined further down in the file, preceded by the label Palette.

```
Palette:
        hex 1f              ;screen color
        hex 01112100        ;background 0
        hex 02122200        ;background 1
        hex 02112100        ;background 2
        hex 01122200        ;background 3
        hex 19293900        ;sprite 0
        hex 1a2a3a00        ;sprite 1
        hex 1b2b3b00        ;sprite 2
        hex 1c2c3c          ;sprite 3
```

The Hello World (ASM) demo only uses the first palette entry (and screen color), but in later chapters, we'll use them all.

35.2 Writing to the Nametable

To draw text to the background, we have to write to a *nametable*. This is similar to writing to palette memory, except with a different PPU address. We need to compute the starting address of our text, which depends on where we want to draw it.

Our emulator doesn't display the left, right, and top 8-pixel borders, as most TVs wouldn't display them anyway. So instead of starting at column 0, row 0, we start at column 1, row 1.

Each row of a nametable has 32 bytes. So to find the address in nametable A, we use this equation:

```
PPU address = 0x2000 + column + (row * 0x20)
```

If `column` and `row` are both 1, this gives us an address of $2021.

Our `HelloVRAM` routine will differ from `SetPalette` in that we don't write a fixed number of bytes. Instead, we stop when we see a zero entry, also known as a *null terminator*. If the LDA instruction sets the 6502's zero flag, the BEQ will exit the loop.

35. Drawing Text in Assembly

```
HelloVRAM: subroutine
; set PPU address to nametable A (row 1, col 1)
        PPU_SETADDR $2021
        ldy #0              ; set Y counter to 0
.loop:
        lda HelloMsg,y      ; get next character
        beq .end            ; is 0? exit loop
        sta PPU_DATA        ; store+advance PPU
        iny                 ; next character
        bne .loop           ; loop
.end:
        rts                 ; return to caller
```

We also have to define our message, using an *ASCII* string. Then we add a byte 0 for the null terminator.

```
HelloMsg:
        .byte "Hello, World!"
        .byte 0             ; zero terminator
```

35.3 Linking the Pattern Table

We also need a *pattern table* to define the bitmaps for our tiles. We're using *CHR ROM*, so it will be hard-coded in the ROM file. The NES file format includes the CHR data after the PRG data. Our *iNES header* defines 2 PRG banks from address $8000 to $FFFF. So the CHR data starts at $10000:

```
        org $10000
        incbin "jroatch.chr"
        incbin "jroatch.chr"
```

The **incbin** directive includes a binary file into the ROM. The .chr extension identifies a CHR pattern table file. Our file is 4096 bytes long, containing 256 tiles.

This doesn't match our iNES header, which specifies one CHR bank for a total of 8192 bytes (512 tiles). Some emulators are picky about this, so we issue **incbin** twice to get the desired CHR ROM length.

 Can you change the message written to the screen? Can you change its position?

36

Scrolling in Assembly

> Open the example on 8bitworkshop.com: From the
> **Platforms** menu, select **Game Consoles » NES**, then
> select the **Scrolling Demo (ASM)** project from the
> Project Selector dropdown.

36.1 Filling up VRAM

This demo scrolls the entire screen. First, we'll fill the entire nametable memory with data. We'll put A characters in nametable A, and B characters in nametable B.

```
FillVRAM: subroutine
        PPU_SETADDR $2000
        ldy #$8         ; set $8 pages ($800 bytes)
.loop:
        lda PageData,y  ; PageData[Y] -> A
        sta PPU_DATA    ; A -> PPU data port
        inx             ; X = X + 1
        bne .loop       ; repeat until 256 bytes
        dey             ; Y = Y - 1
        bne .loop       ; repeat until Y is 0
        rts             ; return to caller
```

The PageData lookup table tells the FillVRAM routine what goes in each 256-byte page.

36. Scrolling in Assembly

Note that it's backwards, because we count down the Y register from 8 to 0:

```
PageData:
        hex 00          ; index 0 not used
        hex 42424242    ; 'B'
        hex 41414141    ; 'A'
```

Each 2x2 square of tiles will be colored in a checkerboard pattern, because we're filling up the *attribute table* with the same $41 and $42 bytes.

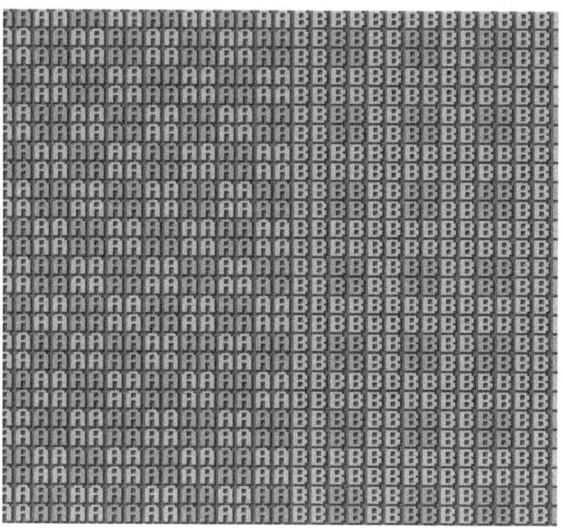

36.2 Scrolling in the NMI Routine

Setting the scrolling registers is typically done during the *NMI* routine, when the PPU is inactive.

- Find the X and Y coordinates of the upper left corner of the visible area (the part seen by the "camera")
- Write the X coordinate to PPU_SCROLL ($2005)
- Write the Y coordinate to PPU_SCROLL
- Write the starting page (high order bit of X and Y) to bits 0 and 1 of PPU_CTRL ($2000)

36.2. Scrolling in the NMI Routine

First, we have to add a variable to hold the horizontal scroll position:

```
ScrollPos       word    ; used during NMI
```

Now we'll write an NMI handler to animate the scroll registers.

The first thing we typically do in an interrupt routine is to save all the registers. The 6502 pushes the Flags register onto the stack when an interrupt fires...but if we use any other register in our interrupt routine, it'll be *clobbered* when it exits, corrupting the rest of our program. So we want to save the A, X, and Y registers, too. This macro pushes them onto the stack:

```
NMIHandler:
        SAVE_REGS       ; save registers onto stack
```

We want to make the screen scroll to the right, so we'll increment the scroll position every frame. While it's a 16-bit quantity, we can only increment one byte at a time. We only increment the second byte if the first byte wraps around to zero:

```
        inc ScrollPos   ; increment low byte
        bne .noinc      ; Z flag set if wrapped to 0
        inc ScrollPos+1 ; increment high byte
.noinc
```

We store the horizontal scroll position by writing to PPU_SCROLL:

```
        lda ScrollPos   ; low byte -> A
        sta PPU_SCROLL  ; set horiz scroll
```

We store the vertical scroll position (always zero in this demo) by writing to the same register:

```
        lda #0          ; zero -> A
        sta PPU_SCROLL  ; set vert scroll
```

This is similar to how we write twice to PPU_ADDR to set the 16-bit PPU address. The first write to PPU_SCROLL stores the X scroll position, the second write stores the Y scroll position. Each write toggles an internal flag, which is shared with PPU_ADDR.

There are 512 possible horizontal scroll positions (256 * 2 nametables) but we only set one 8-bit register, PPU_SCROLL. This

203

36. Scrolling in Assembly

only gives us positions 0-255. For positions 256-511, we need to set the PPU_CTRL register, which contains the eighth bit. This bit chooses nametable A or B for the upper-left corner.

```
; store 8th bit into name table selector
; name table A or B ($2000 or $2400)
lda ScrollPos+1  ; load high byte
and #1           ; select its low bit
ora #CTRL_NMI    ; set rest of bits
sta PPU_CTRL     ; set PPU control register
```

Since we used the SAVE_REGS macro earlier, we must restore the A, X, and Y registers before we return from the interrupt. RESTORE_REGS pops them off the stack in reverse order:

```
RESTORE_REGS     ; restore registers from stack
```

RTI returns from the NMI routine. It pulls the Flags register and Program Counter off of the stack, essentially returning the CPU to what it was doing before the interrupt.

```
rti              ; return from interrupt
```

The PPU_SCROLL and PPU_ADDR registers interact with internal PPU registers. If you need to write to PPU_ADDR in the NMI handler, you should generally do it before writing to PPU_SCROLL, or the scroll position will be wrong. We'll take advantage of this behavior in Chapter 40.

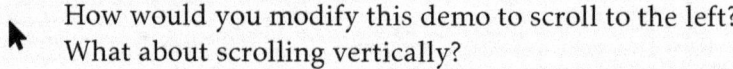

> How would you modify this demo to scroll to the left? What about scrolling vertically?

37

Sprites/OAM in Assembly

37.1 Sprites

Setting up sprites requires writing to the PPU's internal OAM memory.

We could write to OAM via the OAM_ADDR and OAM_DATA registers, much like how we write to video RAM with PPU_ADDR and PPU_DATA. However, this only writes a byte at a time, and is not the preferred method.

Instead, we'll set up the sprites in CPU RAM, and use the *OAMDMA* register to transfer the entire 64-sprite buffer to the PPU, once per frame.

> Open the example on 8bitworkshop.com: From the **Platforms** menu, select **Game Consoles** » **NES**, then select the **Sprite Demo (ASM)** project from the Project Selector dropdown.

Typically, the OAM buffer is set up at addresses $200-$2FF:

```
SpriteBuf      equ     $200
```

37. Sprites/OAM in Assembly

We initialize the OAM buffer by randomizing all values. We call the NextRandom function (in **nesppu.dasm**) to do this:

```
InitSprites: subroutine
            lda #1
            ldx #0
.loop
            sta SpriteBuf,x
            jsr NextRandom
            inx
            bne .loop
            rts
```

The NMI handler for the sprite demo is similar to the one we used in the last chapter — we set the scrolling registers the same way. But in this demo, we also need to draw the sprites.

The PPU_OAM_DMA ($4014) register begins a *DMA* transfer. When this register is written, an entire *page* (256 bytes) of data is copied from CPU RAM to the PPU.

Whatever value is written to the register becomes the high byte of the RAM address. Since our OAM buffer lives at $200-$2FF, we write a $02 to begin the transfer:

```
            lda #$02            ; A = $02
            sta PPU_OAM_DMA     ; copy $200-$2FF to OAM
```

The DMA process begins, and uploads the entire 256 byte buffer to the PPU in 513 or 514 CPU cycles — less than 5 scanlines. The CPU is stalled during this time.

Because the OAM is implemented with *dynamic RAM* inside the PPU, it decays over time. Writing refreshes the memory, so it's a good idea to upload sprites during every frame, even if sprites have not moved.

We also call the MoveSprites routine in our NMI handler. It just adds a number between 0 and 3 to each byte in OAM, which not only makes the sprites move, but also cycles their attributes and tile index.

37.1. Sprites

```
MoveSprites: subroutine
        lda #1          ; A = 1
        ldx #0          ; X = 0
.loop
        sta Temp1           ; save A
        and #3              ; keep lower 2 bits
        clc                 ; clear carry before add
        adc SpriteBuf,x     ; add to sprite buffer
        sta SpriteBuf,x     ; store in sprite buffer
        lda Temp1           ; restore A
        jsr NextRandom      ; get next random number
        inx                 ; X = X + 1
        bne .loop           ; loop until X wraps
        rts                 ; return to caller
```

Even with this simple loop, it still takes about 1.5 scanlines to move each sprite. This is competitive with the *metasprite* functions in NESLib, which are also written in assembly.

▶ How would you make sprites move only in the X or Y direction without changing the attributes or tile index? How would you make them all move at the same speed?

38

Controller Reading in Assembly

Each controller has an associated I/O port:

Hex Addr	Name	Bits Used 76543210	Description
$4016	JOY1	...xxxxd	Joystick 1 (read)
$4017	JOY2	...xxxxd	Joystick 2 (read)

Unlike many systems, the NES does not return all of its controller inputs at once. It continuously reloads the switch values into an internal *shift register*, which can be read one bit at a time. To read all of the controller inputs, the CPU has to poll each controller's I/O port until all bits are read.

You'll find the `ReadJoypad` subroutine in the **nesppu.dasm** file. First, we set the `strobe` bit, which reloads the controller values into the shift register:

```
ReadJoypad subroutine
        lda #$01      ; bit 0 is strobe bit
        sta JOYPAD1   ; set strobe bit in register
```

We then reset the strobe bit, which stops the reloading and freezes the current values:

```
        lsr           ; clever way to set A = 0
        sta JOYPAD1   ; clear strobe bit
```

38. Controller Reading in Assembly

Now we loop eight times, one for each bit in the result. The X register holds our loop count.

```
        ldx #8          ; loop over 8 bits
.loop:
```

Each time we loop, we read the JOYPAD1 register and apply the LSR (logical shift right) instruction. This shifts the lower (rightmost) bit into the Carry register, which is the next controller switch value. Our final result will be stored in A, so we surround these instructions with PHA/PLA instructions to avoid clobbering this register:

```
        pha             ; save A (result)
        lda JOYPAD1     ; load controller state
        lsr             ; bit 0 -> carry
        pla             ; restore A (result)
```

Now that the Carry bit is set with the switch value, we ROL (rotate left) to shift the Carry bit into our result. Then we loop until X is 0, which takes eight iterations.

```
        rol             ; carry -> bit 0 of result
        dex             ; X = X - 1
        bne .loop       ; repeat if X is 0
        rts             ; controller bits returned in A
```

ReadJoypad and ReadJoypad0 return a bitmask in the A register:

Bit Index	Hex Mask	Description
0	0x1	Right
1	0x2	Left
2	0x4	Down
3	0x8	Up
4	0x10	Start
5	0x20	Select
6	0x40	B button
7	0x80	A button

We can test individual buttons like this:

```
jsr ReadJoypad0      ; read joypad 0 mask into A reg
and #$40             ; test B button
bne PressedBtnB      ; branch if pressed (bit set)
```

This code only reads the first controller, but we could modify it to read either controller. We'll use the 6502's *absolute indexed* mode. Every instruction that references JOYPAD1 we'll change to read JOYPAD1,y, for example:

```
lda JOYPAD1,y    ; load controller[Y] state
```

Then we can set the Y register to either 0 (first controller) or 1 (second controller) before calling ReadJoypad.

> Open the example on 8bitworkshop.com: From the **Platforms** menu, select **Game Consoles » NES**, then select the **Controller Demo (ASM)** project from the Project Selector dropdown.

In the demo, we read the joypad in the NMI handler. We scroll the background layer in the direction that the joypad is pressed.

To calculate the offset to add to the scroll registers, we use a four-entry lookup table:

```
ScrollDirTab:
        hex 00 01 ff 00      ; 0,1,-1,0
```

We mask two bits of the joypad mask for each axis (left/right and up/down), giving us a range of 0 to 3. We use this index to look up the offset in the lookup table.

We'll use this lookup table in the NMI handler for both X and Y axes.

38. Controller Reading in Assembly

Here's the code for the X axis:

```
jsr ReadJoypad0        ; read first controller
pha                    ; push joypad bitmask
and #$03               ; only keep first 2 bits
tay                    ; A -> Y
lda ScrollDirTab,y     ; lookup table
clc                    ; clear carry flag
adc ScrollX            ; compute A + ScrollX
sta ScrollX            ; -> ScrollX
sta PPU_SCROLL         ; -> first scroll byte
```

Note that we used the PHA instruction to push the joypad mask onto the stack. After computing the new X scroll position, we use PLA to pull it back into the A register and compute the Y axis:

```
  pla               ; pull joypad bitmask
  lsr               ; shift right two bits
  lsr               ; to get up/down switches
;  ...              the rest is similar to X axis
```

Note that each call to ReadJoypad routine takes several CPU cycles to complete — about two scanlines. It's best to call it no more than once per frame per controller.

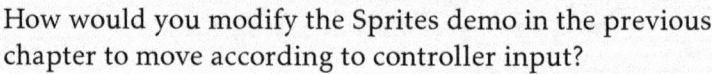

You may notice that the screen sometimes jumps when scrolling up or down. This is because the Y position wraps from 255 to 0 (or vice-versa) and the nametable is only 240 lines high. How would you fix this?

How would you modify the Sprites demo in the previous chapter to move according to controller input?

39

FamiTone and DMC Samples

> Open the example on 8bitworkshop.com: From the
> **Platforms** menu, select **Game Consoles » NES**, then
> select the **FamiTone Demo (ASM)** project from the
> Project Selector dropdown.

Initializing the FamiTone2 music library in assembler is a little more complex, but not too difficult. You have to pass a parameter to FamiToneInit that tells it if you're on NTSC or PAL, as this affects the NMI rate (60 Hz vs 50 Hz):

```
ldx #<music_data
ldy #>music_data         ; get music data address in X/Y
lda PPU_STATUS           ; get PPU status byte
and #$80                 ; isolate NTSC mode bit
eor #$80                 ; invert it
jsr FamiToneInit         ; initialize famitone
lda #0                   ; A <- 0
jsr FamiToneMusicPlay    ; play song #0
```

In your NMI handler, you just have place a call to FamiToneUpdate, preferably near the end after your PPU writes are complete.

39.1 APU DMC Sound

The APU can output sampled audio using a technique called *delta modulation*. There is a 7-bit counter that is connected

39. FAMITONE AND DMC SAMPLES

Figure 39.1: DMC sample generation. 1=up, 0=down

to a *digital-analog converter* (DAC). The value of this counter determines the *amplitude* (level, or height) of the waveform.

Meanwhile, the *DMC* (Delta Modulation Channel) reads a stream of bits from the CPU, each bit generating a new sample. If the bit is set, the counter is incremented. If the bit is clear, the counter is decremented.

By clever encoding of these bits, a waveform is generated that approximates the original audio. The resulting sound is somewhat fuzzy, but the space savings are enormous compared to *PCM* encoding, which stores the full value of each sample.

The FamiTone2 library supports DMC sample generation in music and in sound effects. They are often used for drum sounds or other short sound effects. The DMC samples must be placed at a 64-byte-aligned address at $C000 or higher.

It's easier to demonstrate this with assembly code. Here, we put our sample data at address $F000 using the ORG directive:

```
        org     $f000
DMCSamples
        hex     a97ee93ffc3ff00f0700000000000000
        ...
FT_DPCM_OFF     = DMCSamples    ;$c000..$ffc0, 64-byte steps
FT_DPCM_ENABLE  = 1             ;undefine to exclude DMC code
```

The FT_DPCM_OFF constant tells the FamiTone2 library at which address the samples can be found.

40

Split Screen X/Y Scrolling

In Chapter 36, we learned that we can change the background scroll position by setting the PPU_SCROLL register twice — the first time for the X position, and the second time for the Y position. We also set the high-order bits of the scroll position in PPU_CTRL.

This works fine when the PPU is inactive, or during the vertical blank period. We can even set the X scroll position while the frame is being drawn, if we make our changes before the end of the line. This is how we do screen splits, after waiting for sprite zero or an IRQ.

However, if the PPU is active, this will not change the vertical scroll position. The PPU's internal registers that determine the vertical position are refreshed at the end of the line, and changes will be ignored.

There is a way to change both X and Y scroll positions during a screen split, but it's more complicated.

> ▸ Open the example on 8bitworkshop.com: From the **Platforms** menu, select **Game Consoles » NES**, then select the **XY Split Scrolling** project from the Project Selector dropdown.

40. Split Screen X/Y Scrolling

40.1 VRAM Address Registers

The PPU has two internal 15-bit registers that affect scrolling. One is the *current VRAM address*, set when writing to PPU_ADDR, and modified while the PPU fetches tile data. The other is the *temporary VRAM address*, also called the *Nametable Start Address*.

When setting the X scroll position (the first write to PPU_SCROLL), the temporary VRAM address and fine X register is updated like so:

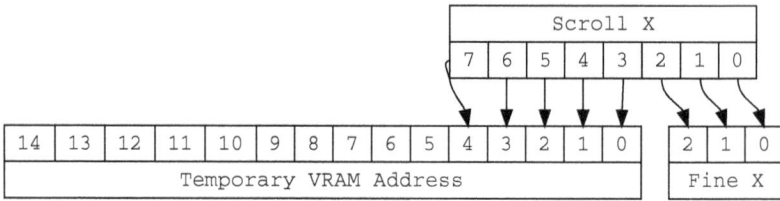

The Y scroll position (the second write to PPU_SCROLL) updates it like so (note the Y fine position stored in the high-order bits):

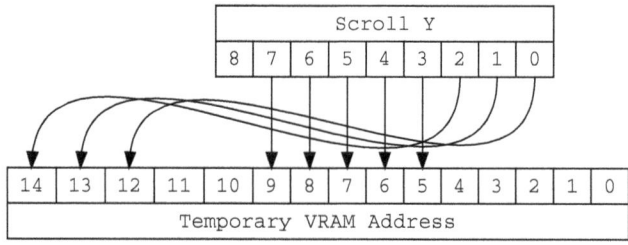

Before each video frame begins, the bits that relate to vertical scrolling are copied from the temporary VRAM address to the current VRAM address:

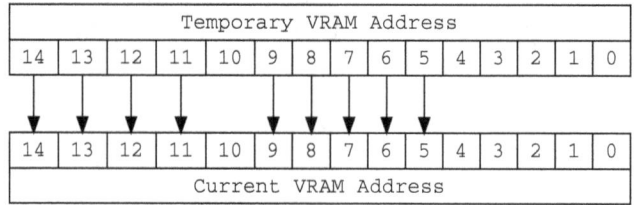

40.2. Setting Y Scroll During Rendering

There's also a 3-bit *fine X scroll* register which is set during the first write to PPU_SCROLL. The fine Y scroll value is actually kept in the high three bits of the temporary VRAM address, since the PPU only uses the first 11 bits for addressing.

Setting the PPU_SCROLL register updates the fine X scroll register and the temporary VRAM address immediately. After the PPU draws a scanline, it copies the bits that relate to horizontal scrolling from the temporary VRAM address to the current VRAM address:

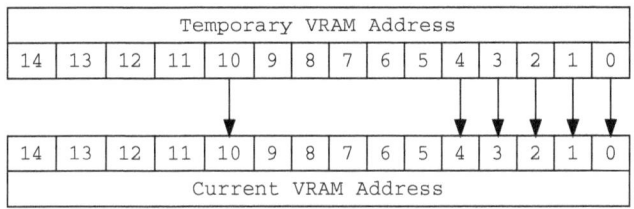

40.2 Setting Y Scroll During Rendering

To affect Y scroll position during a split, we must set both the current and temporary VRAM addresses, via the PPU_SCROLL and PPU_ADDR registers. We must write to these registers in a certain order, in four separate writes. The outcome of this sequence of writes is illustrated below:

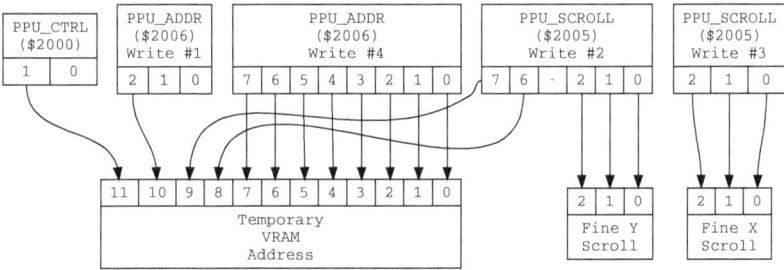

The second write to PPU_ADDR goes directly into the VRAM address, so it has components of both the X and Y scroll position. We need to compute this value:

PPU_ADDR.2 = (ScrollX >> 3) | ((ScrollY & 0x38) << 2)

40. Split Screen X/Y Scrolling

The sequence of writes must take place quickly, so we precompute this value and push it to the stack:

```
; compute second PPU_ADDR write
        lda ScrollX
        tax             ; ScrollX -> X
        lsr
        lsr
        lsr
        sta Temp
        lda ScrollY
        tay             ; ScrollY -> Y
        and #$38
        asl
        asl
        ora Temp        ; (ScrollX>>3) | ((ScrollY&0x38)<<2)
        pha             ; push onto stack
```

We wait for the sprite zero hit, by polling PPU_STATUS:

```
; wait for sprite 0
.wait0  bit PPU_STATUS
        bvs .wait0
.wait1  bit PPU_STATUS
        bvc .wait1
```

Now we quickly perform our sequence of writes. The first is a write to PPU_ADDR, which sets the high bit of the X scroll position when the value is 256 or higher. We don't use it in this demo, so we set it to zero.

```
; set PPU_ADDR.1
        lda #0
        sta PPU_ADDR
```

This write does change the upper/lower flag, which is shared by PPU_SCROLL. So our next two writes will affect the Y scroll position first, then the X scroll position:

```
; set PPU_SCROLL.1
        sty PPU_SCROLL      ; set Y scroll bits
; set PPU_SCROLL.2
        stx PPU_SCROLL      ; set X scroll bits
```

(That the registers are named Y and X are pure coincidence!)

40.2. Setting Y Scroll During Rendering

Our last write is to PPU_ADDR. We computed it earlier, so we pull it from the stack:

```
; set PPU_ADDR.2
    pla
    sta PPU_ADDR
```

This example doesn't set the nametable select bit in PPU_CTRL. How you'd handle this differs depending on the nametable mirroring setting.

This seems pretty tricky, no? For C developers, there's a **splitxy()** function in NESLib that does this. It's as easy as:

```
splitxy(x, y);        // perform X and Y split
```

The exact timing is more critical than the standard horizontal-only **split()** function. You may have to tweak the horizontal position of sprite zero to get it to work on more fussy emulators.

In the XY Split Scrolling demo, all four PPU writes occur after pixel 257 of the scanline. We'll explain more about scanline timing in the next chapter.

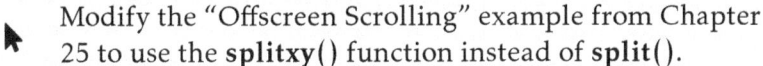 Modify the "Offscreen Scrolling" example from Chapter 25 to use the **splitxy()** function instead of **split()**.

41

Line-by-line Scrolling

The NES was designed for 2D graphics. Nevertheless, game developers learned how to "fake it," giving players the impression of 3D graphics using 2D techniques. This is often referred to as *pseudo-3D*, or "2.5D." It's more art than science, using color, shape, and animation to fool the eye into perceiving depth.

We start by drawing a 3D perspective view of a road into two side-by-side nametables. This is tricky, so we use the **makechr** utility.[1] It converts a PNG bitmap into a full graphics set: pattern table, nametable, attribute table, and palette.

Figure 41.1: Side-by-side nametable for road demo.

---

[1] https://dustmop.io/software/makechr

41. Line-by-line Scrolling

The source PNG has to be specially crafted to fit the constraints of the NES. For example, each 8x8 tile can have no more than three colors, plus the screen background color. This is why the details disappear close to the horizon, because there are too many colors to fit into a single tile. There is also a limit to the pattern table size, which is why the mountains are only eight pixels high.

Once we draw the road image into a PNG, we run **makechr** to generate the NES-compatible files. In our code, we include them using the **incbin** directive:

```
RoadTables:
        incbin "road/nametable.dat"
        incbin "road/attribute.dat"
        incbin "road/nametable1.dat"
        incbin "road/attribute1.dat"

        org $10000
        incbin "road/road.chr"
```

We need at least two copies of the palette to perform *color cycling*:

```
Palette:
        hex 0F3F06300F19063F0F1916063F180801
        hex 0F30163F0F19163F0F1906160F180801
```

Before each frame, we might switch between the two palettes, depending on the speed of the player. This gives the illusion of the curbing and lane stripes zooming by.

```
        lda TPos              ; track position
        lsr                   ; / 2
        and #16               ; now either 0 or 16
        tay                   ; Y is palette offset
        jsr SetPalette        ; call SetPalette
        PPU_SETADDR $2000     ; reset PPU address
```

41.1 Scanline Manipulation

For special effects like a 3D road, we may want to manipulate the scroll register for each individual scanline. We could use

41.1. Scanline Manipulation

MMC3 IRQs, but the overhead of each interrupt would be significant. Instead, we will carefully time the CPU instructions so that we modify the PPU registers at the right time during each scanline.

During each scanline, the PPU counts out 341 *pixel clocks*, each roughly corresponding to a pixel. Only the first 256 are visible. The PPU has a predictable sequence of VRAM reads:

Pixel Clock
- 1-248   Fetch background (nametable, attribute table, pattern table)
- 249-256   Unused tile fetch
- 257-320   Fetch sprites (OAM, pattern table)
- 321-340   Fetch first two tiles for next scanline

And a predictable series of internal operations:

Pixel Clock
- 0-256   Increment X address
- 256   Increment Y address
- 257   Reload X address from temporary
- 280-304   Reload Y address from temporary
- 328-340   Increment X address

As you can see, there's a lot going on, and we may get glitches if we mess with registers at the wrong times. Updating PPU_SCROLL changes the fine X scroll immediately, so we can't do it during the visible scanline. If we do it after pixel 256, the PPU address reloads might conflict with our updates.

In this demo, we'll try to update the PPU registers between pixel 249 and 255 during the unused tile fetches. But it's tricky to get the timing exactly right on every scanline.

> ▶ Open the example on 8bitworkshop.com: From the **Platforms** menu, select **Game Consoles » NES**, then select the **3-D Road Demo** project from the Project Selector dropdown.

41. Line-by-line Scrolling

We'll do this demo in assembly code. First, we set up a *sprite zero* split, writing to the OAM buffer:

```
SetSprite0: subroutine
        sta $200        ; A reg -> Y position
        lda #$01
        sta $201        ; #$01 -> tile index
        lda #$20
        sta $202        ; #$20 -> flags
        lda #$fe
        sta $203        ; #$fe -> X position
        rts

        lda #110        ; #110 -> A
        jsr SetSprite0  ; set sprite 0 in OAM buffer
        lda #$02
        sta PPU_OAM_DMA ; copy $200-$2FF to OAM
```

Sprite zero starts on line 109, just above the horizon. We use the time before the split to calculate the road segments and the X position of each scanline containing the road.

Now we wait for the sprite zero flag, which fast-forwards the PPU to the desired scanline:

```
; wait for sprite 0
.wait0  bit PPU_STATUS
        bvs .wait0
.wait1  bit PPU_STATUS
        bvc .wait1
```

After the second loop exits, there's a degree of uncertainty as to which pixel clock the PPU will be working on. This is called *jitter*. Our loop has about seven CPU cycles of jitter, which means if our target PPU pixel is 235, it might be as high as 255.

Now we go into our scanline loop. For each iteration, we look up the horizontal scroll register value in a RAM array and set the PPU_SCROLL register.

```
        ldy #0
.loop
        SLEEP 80        ; ensure 114 CPU cycles/iteration
        tya             ; Y -> A
        lsr             ; A / 2
        tax             ; A -> X
        lda RoadX0,x    ; get X offset of scanline
        eor #$80        ; + 128
        sta PPU_SCROLL  ; horiz byte (1st byte)
        sta PPU_SCROLL  ; vert byte (2nd byte)
        iny
        cpy #NumRoadScanlines
        bne .loop       ; do next scanline
```

We want to time the second write to PPU_SCROLL so that it's between pixel clocks 235 and 255, accounting for jitter.

41.2 A More Accurate Loop

We use the SLEEP macro to add no-operation cycles before repeating the loop. This pads out each loop iteration to exactly 114 CPU cycles.

There's a problem, though. If you were to click **Run to Line** on one of these instructions and view the PPU tab in the Debug Info window, you'll see that the PPU's X coordinate shifts by one every scanline.

This is because on the NES, a scanline actually takes 113 ⅔ CPU cycles (on NTSC systems, that is) and our loop takes 114 cycles. So if we take out one cycle every third scanline, we'll be exactly synced to the PPU's scanline.

We need a counter that we can reset every three scanlines. We'll call it NMITmp:

```
        lda #3
        sta NMITmp      ; count every 3 lines
```

We'll decrement the counter every scanline. When it hits zero, we'll branch outside the loop to reset it:

```
        dec NMITmp      ; decrement 3-line counter
        beq .resetx     ; has it been 3 lines?
```

41. Line-by-line Scrolling

This consumes nine CPU cycles whenever we reset the counter, so we have to loop to a different branch entry point (.skipcyc) that returns ten cycles, because the whole goal was to save one cycle every three scanlines:

```
        SLEEP 10        ; only run if counter not reset
.skipcyc
        SLEEP 70        ; always run
```

This loop requires exact accounting of CPU cycles. We must ensure that none of our branches cross a page (256-byte) boundary, which would add extra cycles.

Often a lot of fiddling is required to minimize graphical glitches. Figure 41.2 shows a debugging tool being used to check the timing of PPU register writes.

> The **JSNES** emulator is more forgiving of scroll register timing issues, so you should check this kind of code on high-quality emulators like **Mesen** and **fceux**.

Figure 41.2: PPU Event Viewer in the Mesen emulator. The vertical lines on the right side of the road show the timing of PPU register writes. The dots above the horizon are PPU status reads while waiting for sprite zero.

42

NES Dev Tools

42.1 8bitworkshop Asset Editor

The **8bitworkshop IDE** has a built-in **Asset Editor** that allows you to edit some game resources. Make sure the left side of the IDE is expanded, and click the **Asset Editor** link.

The Asset Editor scans your code, looking for special *comment tags*. It parses the arrays into editable assets, like bitmaps and palettes. They'll show up in the Asset Editor, and changes you make there will change the original source files, modifying the hex values in the associated array.

An assembly source file can be tagged with ";;" comments — for example, a pattern table:

`;;{w:8,h:8,bpp:1,count:256,brev:1,np:2,pofs:8,remap:[...]};;`

A C source file can be tagged with a /* */ comment — here's a palette tag:

`/*{pal:"nes",layout:"nes"}*/`

The {...} braces enclose *JSON* objects, which tell the Asset Editor details about the array data that follows.

There are more examples scattered through the sample code in the IDE. To make a new asset, just cut-and-paste the array including the preceding comment, and modify the new version.

42.2 Other Tools

For more advanced asset creation and editing, some useful third-party tools include:

NES Screen Tool   https://shiru.untergrund.net/

A Windows tool for editing NES nametables, attributes, palettes, patterns (tiles), and metasprites. It can export *RLE*-encoded nametables, which we discussed in Chapter 24.

YY-CHR   https://www.romhacking.net/utilities/119/

Another popular Windows CHR graphics and nametable editor.

makechr   https://github.com/dustmop/makechr

Automatically creates NES-format graphics (tilesets, nametables, palettes, and sprites) from a 256x240 bitmap.

To install on Linux/OSX: `pip install makechr`

FamiTracker   http://famitracker.com/

FamiTracker is a free Windows tracker for producing music for the NES/Famicom systems. It exports source code which can be played using the *FamiTone2* library. We discussed this in Chapter 22.

fceux   http://www.fceux.com/

An accurate NES/Famicom emulator for Windows and Linux/OSX/etc via SDL. FCEUX offers tools for debugging, map making, tool-assisted movies, and Lua scripting. Some of these features might only be available on Windows.

Mesen   https://www.mesen.ca/

A high-accuracy NES and Famicom emulator and NSF player for Windows and Linux. Cross-platform debugging UI written in C#.

NESICIDE https://github.com/christopherpow/nesicide

A multiplatform IDE that integrates with a NES emulator and **FamiTracker**. You can program both C and assembler with the **cc65/cc65** toolchain.

NesDev   http://nesdev.com/

A website with message boards dedicated to helping NES developers and reviewing homebrew games.

NESASM and **ASM6** are alternate 6502 assemblers that you might run across while browsing the source code for NES homebrew games. You'll have to translate the code to **DASM** dialect to use it in the IDE.

And of course, **NESLib** is the code library from Alex 'Shiru' Semenov that we've been using this entire time for C programming. You can find the fork used by the **8bitworkshop IDE** here:

https://github.com/sehugg/neslib

Shiru's original code can be found at:

https://shiru.unterground.net/code.shtml

42.3 Making Your Own Homebrew Game

You might decide to tackle a complete game project. There are lots of decisions to make, among them:

How to represent the game world? Should you store levels as RLE-compressed nametables designed with NES Screen Tool, or something else? Should you make your own level format and your own design tools?

What kind of mirroring? This depends on whether your primary scroll direction is horizontal or vertical, and how you want to hide offscreen artifacts.

CHR ROM or RAM? A single CHR ROM bank is good enough for simple games. Multiple CHR ROM banks can give you different graphics for each level and/or animation effects, and can be switched quickly. A CHR RAM system gives you more flexibility, but is more complex to manage and slow to update.

8x8 or 8x16 sprites? The former allows more small objects, but the latter allows you to use all 512 tiles in the pattern table and can save CPU time since there are fewer entries for large metasprites.

How many actors on-screen at once? As your game gets more complex, CPU time gets scarce. For example, the Climber game can only display about seven or eight actors at once before the frame rate starts to stutter.

How to interact with the game world? For example, how will the game code detect collisions between actors and the world? How will new actors spawn and be culled when offscreen? Doing design work up-front to make this efficient can save you scrambling in the long run.

How big is your ROM? If you want to have a huge game world or lots of levels with complex rules, you might as well plan for *bank switching* ahead of time.

If you want to share your source code, you can publish it to GitHub right from the **8bitworkshop IDE**. We've got a homebrew showcase at `http://8bitworkshop.com/projects`.

In any case, feel free to tell us about your programming adventure at `info@8bitworkshop.com`!

Good Luck!

Appendix A: NES Reference

Start	End	Description
$0000	$00FF	RAM, zero-page
$0100	$01FF	RAM, CPU stack
$0200	$07FF	RAM, general-purpose
$0800	$1FFF	(mirror of $0000-$07FF)
$2000	$2007	PPU registers
$2008	$3FFF	(mirror of $2000-$2007)
$4000	$400F	APU registers
$4010	$4017	DMC, joystick, APU registers
$4020	$5FFF	Cartridge (maybe mapper registers)
$6000	$7FFF	Cartridge RAM (maybe battery-backed)
$8000	$FFFF	PRG ROM (maybe bank switched)
$FFFA	$FFFB	NMI vector
$FFFC	$FFFD	Reset vector
$FFFE	$FFFF	BRK vector

Table 1: NES CPU Memory Map

Address Range	Description
$0000-$0FFF	Pattern Table 0
$1000-$1FFF	Pattern Table 1
$2000-$23BF / $23C0-$23FF	Name Table 0 / Attribute Table 0
$2400-$27BF / $27C0-$27FF	Name Table 1 / Attribute Table 1
$2800-$2BBF / $2BC0-$2BFF	Name Table 2 / Attribute Table 2
$2C00-$2FBF / $2FC0-$2FFF	Name Table 3 / Attribute Table 3
$3F00-$3F0F / $3F10-$3F1F	Background Palettes / Sprite Palettes
Internal OAM Memory	64 Sprites (256 bytes)

Figure 1: NES PPU Memory Map

Appendix A: NES Reference

Hex Addr	Name	Read/ Write	Description
$2000	PPU_CTRL	write	PPU Control 1
$2001	PPU_MASK	write	PPU Control 2
$2002	PPU_STATUS	read	PPU Status
$2003	OAM_ADDR	write	OAM Address
$2004	OAM_DATA	read/write	OAM Data
$2005	PPU_SCROLL	write 2x	Background Scroll Position (write X then Y)
$2006	PPU_ADDR	write 2x	PPU Address (write upper then lower)
$2007	PPU_DATA	read/write	PPU Data
$4014	OAM_DMA	write	Sprite Page DMA Transfer

Table 2: PPU/Graphics Registers

Bit Index	Hex Mask	Description
0-1	0x3	Nametable page select (0=$2000, 1=$2400, 2=$2800, 3=$2c00)
2	0x4	VRAM address increment (0=1, 1=32)
3	0x8	8x8 sprite pattern address (0=$0, 1=$1000)
4	0x10	Background pattern address (0=$0, 1=$1000)
5	0x20	Sprite size (0=8x8, 1=8x16)
6	0x40	Master/slave mode (unused)
7	0x80	NMI enable at VBLANK (0=off, 1=on)

Table 3: PPU_CTRL Bits

Bit Index	Hex Mask	Description
0	0x1	Greyscale (0=color, 1=greyscale)
1	0x2	Show background in leftmost 8 pixels
2	0x4	Show sprites in leftmost 8 pixels
3	0x8	Show background
4	0x10	Show sprites
5	0x20	Red emphasis
6	0x40	Green emphasis
7	0x80	Blue emphasis

Table 4: PPU_MASK Bits

Bit Index	Hex Mask	Description
5	0x20	Sprite overflow (more than 8 on a scanline)
6	0x40	Sprite 0 intersects background
7	0x80	Vertical blank has started (resets after read)

Table 5: PPU_STATUS Bits

Start	End	Description
$3F00	$3F00	Screen color
$3F01	$3F03	Background palette 0
$3F05	$3F07	Background palette 1
$3F09	$3F0B	Background palette 2
$3F0D	$3F0F	Background palette 3
$3F11	$3F13	Sprite palette 0
$3F15	$3F17	Sprite palette 1
$3F19	$3F1B	Sprite palette 2
$3F1D	$3F1F	Sprite palette 3

Table 6: Palette registers

Byte Offset	Description
0	Y coordinate
1	Tile index
2	Attributes
3	X coordinate

Table 7: Sprite OAM Record

Bit Index	Hex Mask	C Expression	Description
0-1	0x3	*integer*	Palette select (0-3)
5	0x20	OAM_BEHIND	Sprite under background
6	0x40	OAM_FLIP_H	Flip pixels horizontally
7	0x80	OAM_FLIP_V	Flip pixels vertically

Table 8: Sprite Attribute Bits

Appendix A: NES Reference

Hex Addr	Name	Bits Used 76543210	Description
$4000	SQ1_VOL	ddlcvvvv	Square wave 1, duty and volume
$4001	SQ1_SWEEP	epppnsss	Square wave 1, sweep
$4002	SQ1_LO	pppppppp	Square wave 1, period (LSB)
$4003	SQ1_HI	xxxxxppp	Square wave 1, period (MSB) and counter load
$4004	SQ2_VOL	dd..vvvv	Square wave 2, duty and volume
$4005	SQ2_SWEEP	epppnsss	Square wave 2, sweep
$4006	SQ2_LO	pppppppp	Square wave 2, period (LSB)
$4007	SQ2_HI	xxxxxppp	Square wave 2, period (MSB) and counter load
$4008	TRI_LINEAR	crrrrrrr	Triangle wave, control and counter load
$400A	TRI_LO	pppppppp	Triangle wave, period (LSB)
$400B	TRI_HI	xxxxxppp	Triangle wave, period (MSB) and counter load
$400C	NOISE_VOL	..lcvvvv	Noise generator, flags and volume
$400E	NOISE_CTRL	t...pppp	Noise generator, tone and period
$400F	NOISE_LEN	lllll...	Noise generator, counter load
$4010	DMC_FREQ	il..rrrr	DMC: IRQ, flags, and rate
$4011	DMC_RAW	.xxxxxxx	DMC: direct load
$4012	DMC_START	aaaaaaaa	DMC, waveform start address
$4013	DMC_LEN	llllllll	DMC, waveform length
$4015	SND_CHN	...dnt21	Sound channel enable
$4017	JOY2	mi......	Frame counter mode and IRQ
$4015	SND_CHN	if.dnt21	DMC/frame interrupt and status (read)
$4016	JOY1	...xxxxd	Joystick 1 (read)
$4017	JOY2	...xxxxd	Joystick 2 (read)

Table 9: APU/Sound/Joystick Registers

Appendix B: NES Colors

Hex	+0	+1	+2	+3
0	gray	blue	mediumblue	slateblue
4	darkmagenta	darkred	darkred	darkred
8	maroon	green	darkgreen	darkgreen
c	teal	(INVALID)	black	black
10	silver	dodgerblue	dodgerblue	mediumslateblue
14	fuchsia	crimson	orangered	chocolate
18	darkgoldenrod	green	green	teal
1c	darkcyan	black	black	black
20	whitesmoke	dodgerblue	cornflowerblue	mediumslateblue
24	violet	hotpink	coral	sandybrown
28	orange	greenyellow	limegreen	palegreen
2c	darkturquoise	gray	black	black
30	white	lightskyblue	lightskyblue	lavender
34	violet	lightpink	palegoldenrod	navajowhite
38	khaki	khaki	palegreen	paleturquoise
3c	aqua	linen	black	black

Appendix C: NESLib Reference

Function	Description
pal_col(index,color)	Set the color of a palette entry.
pal_bg(*data)	Set the background palette from a 16-byte array.
pal_spr(*data)	Set the sprite palette from a 16-byte array.
pal_all(*data)	Set the background and sprite palettes from a 32-byte array.
pal_clear()	Reset all palette colors to black.
pal_bright(level)	Set virtual bright level (0=black, 4=normal, 8=white)
pal_bg_bright(level)	Set virtual bright level for background only.
pal_spr_bright(level)	Set virtual bright level for sprites only.
ppu_wait_nmi()	Wait for next NMI (60 Hz)
ppu_wait_frame()	Wait for next NMI, but skips frames in NTSC to achieve 50 Hz.
ppu_off()	Turn off PPU rendering.
ppu_on_all()	Turn on background and sprites.
ppu_on_bg()	Turn on background only.
ppu_on_spr()	Turn on sprites only.
ppu_mask(mask)	Set PPU_MASK directly.
ppu_system()	Returns zero for PAL, non-zero for NTSC.
nesclock()	Returns 8-bit counter incremented at every NMI.
get_ppu_ctrl_var()	Get the internal PPU_CTRL variable.
set_ppu_ctrl_var(v)	Set the internal PPU_CTRL variable.
oam_clear()	Clear OAM sprite buffer.
oam_size(size)	Set 0 for 8x8 sprites, 1 for 8x16 sprites.
oam_spr(x,y,c,a,id)	Add sprite entry to OAM.
oam_meta_spr(x,y,id,*data)	Add metasprite to OAM.

Appendix C: NESLib Reference

Function	Description
oam_hide_rest(id)	Hide OAM entries starting from given index.
famitone_init(*data)	Initialize FamiTone music library.
sfx_init(*data)	Initialize FamiTone sound effects.
music_play(index)	Play a FamiTone song.
music_stop()	Stop music.
music_pause()	Pause and unpause music.
sfx_play(index,channel)	Play sound effect on channel 0-3.
sample_play(sample)	Play a DMC sample.
famitone_update()	Called once per NMI.
pad_poll(pad)	Poll controller input.
pad_trigger(pad)	Poll in trigger mode.
pad_state(pad)	Get previously polled pad state.
scroll(x,y)	Set X and Y scroll shadow registers.
split(x,y)	Split screen at Y position (requires sprite 0 setup first). Only sets the X scroll value.
splitxy(x,y)	Split screen, setting both X and Y scroll values.
bank_bg(n)	Set background CHR bank (0 or 1).
bank_spr(n)	Set sprite CHR bank (0 or 1).
vram_adr(adr)	Set PPU VRAM address.
vram_put(n)	Write a byte to VRAM.
vram_fill(n,len)	Write len copies of byte n.
vram_inc(n)	Set auto-increment (0=+1, 1=+32)
vram_read(*dst,size)	Read a block of size bytes from VRAM to dst.
vram_write(*src,size)	Write a block of size bytes from src to VRAM.
vram_unrle(*data)	Unpack RLE data to VRAM.
vram_unlz4(*data)	Unpack LZ4 data to VRAM.
set_vram_update(*buf)	Enable VRAM buffer updates with buffer buf.
flush_vram_update(*buf)	Flush VRAM buffer to PPU immediately.
delay(frames)	Delay a number of frames.
nmi_set_callback(*func)	Set the NMI callback function.

Appendix D: C Library Reference

Header	Function
cc65.h	cc65_idiv32by16r16 (rhs, lhs)
cc65.h	cc65_udiv32by16r16 (rhs, lhs)
cc65.h	cc65_imul8x8r16 (lhs, rhs)
cc65.h	cc65_imul16x16r32 (lhs, rhs)
cc65.h	cc65_umul8x8r16 (lhs, rhs)
cc65.h	cc65_umul16x8r32 (lhs, rhs)
cc65.h	cc65_umul16x16r32 (lhs, rhs)
cc65.h	cc65_sin (x)
cc65.h	cc65_cos (x)
ctype.h	isalnum (c)
ctype.h	isalpha (c)
ctype.h	iscntrl (c)
ctype.h	isdigit (c)
ctype.h	isgraph (c)
ctype.h	islower (c)
ctype.h	ispr(c)
ctype.h	ispunct (c)
ctype.h	isspace (c)
ctype.h	isupper (c)
ctype.h	isxdigit (c)
ctype.h	isblank (c)
ctype.h	toupper (c)
ctype.h	tolower (c)
ctype.h	toascii (c)
stdio.h	sprintf (buf, format, args...)
stdio.h	scanf (str, format, args...)
stdlib.h	malloc (size)
stdlib.h	calloc (count, size)
stdlib.h	realloc (block, size)
stdlib.h	free (block)
stdlib.h	srand (seed)
stdlib.h	abs (val)
stdlib.h	labs (val)

Header	Function
stdlib.h	atol (s)
stdlib.h	atexit (*exitfunc)
stdlib.h	bsearch (key, base, n, size, *compfunc)
stdlib.h	div (numer, denom)
stdlib.h	exit (code)
stdlib.h	qsort (base, count, size, *compfunc)
stdlib.h	strtol (nptr, **endptr, base)
stdlib.h	strtoul (nptr, **endptr, base)
stdlib.h	itoa (val, buf, radix)
stdlib.h	utoa (val, buf, radix)
stdlib.h	ltoa (val, buf, radix)
stdlib.h	ultoa (val, buf, radix)
string.h	strcat (dest, src)
string.h	strchr (s, c)
string.h	strcmp (s1, s2)
string.h	strcpy (dest, src)
string.h	strlen (s)
string.h	strncat (s1, s2, count)
string.h	strncmp (s1, s2, count)
string.h	strncpy (dest, src, count)
string.h	strrchr (s, c)
string.h	strspn (s1, s2)
string.h	strstr (str, substr)
string.h	strtok (s1, s2)
string.h	memchr (mem, c, count)
string.h	memcmp (p1, p2, count)
string.h	memcpy (dest, src, count)
string.h	memmove (dest, src, count)
string.h	memset (s, c, count)
string.h	bzero (ptr, n)
string.h	strdup (s)
string.h	stricmp (s1, s2)
string.h	strcasecmp (s1, s2)
string.h	strnicmp (s1, s2, count)
string.h	strncasecmp (s1, s2, count)
string.h	strlower (s)
string.h	strupper (s)

Appendix E: 6502 Instruction Flags

Summary of Documented 6502 Instructions

Mnemonic	Flags Affected	Expression
ADC	NZCV	A += opr
AND	NZ	A &= opr
ASL	NZC	opr <<= 1
BCC	-	branch if C==0
BCS	-	branch if C==1
BEQ	-	branch if Z==0
BIT	NZV	(A & opr); V = bit 6
BMI	-	branch if N==1
BNE	-	branch if Z==1
BRK	B	–
BVC	-	branch if V==0
BVS	-	branch if V==1
CLC	C	C = 0
CLD	D	D = 0
CLV	V	V = 0
CMP	NZC	(A - opr)
CPX	NZC	(X - opr)
CPY	NZC	(Y - opr)
DEC	NZ	opr -= 1
DEX	NZ	X -= 1
DEY	NZ	Y -= 1
EOR	NZ	A ^= opr
INC	NZ	opr += 1
INX	NZ	X += 1
INY	NZ	Y += 1
JMP	-	PC = opr
JSR	-	push PC-1; PC = opr
LDA	NZ	A = opr
LDX	NZ	X = opr
LDY	NZ	Y = opr
LSR	NZC	A >>= 1

Appendix E: 6502 Instruction Flags

Summary of Documented 6502 Instructions

Mnemonic	Flags Affected	Expression
NOP	-	–
PHA	-	[S--] = A
PHP	-	[S--] = P
PLA	NZ	A = [++S]
PLP	all	P = [++S]
ORA	NZ	A |= opr
ROL	NZC	A = (A<<1) | C
ROR	NZC	A = (A>>1) | (C*128)
SBC	NZCV	A -= opr
SEC	C	C = 1
SED	D	D = 1
STA	-	opr = A
STX	-	opr = X
STY	-	opr = Y
TAX	NZ	X = A
TAY	NZ	Y = A
TXA	NZ	A = X
TYA	NZ	A = Y
TSX	NZ	X = S
TXS	NZ	S = X

N = Negative when result >= 128 (high bit set)
Z = Zero when result is 0
C = Carry when addition overflows or bit shifted out
V = Overflow when signed result overflows
D = Decimal (not used in NES)

Appendix F: Powers of Two

Power	Hex	Decimal	Binary
2^0	$1	1	1
2^1	$2	2	10
2^2	$4	4	100
2^3	$8	8	1000
2^4	$10	16	10000
2^5	$20	32	100000
2^6	$40	64	1000000
2^7	$80	128	10000000
2^8	$100	256	100000000
2^9	$200	512	1000000000
2^{10}	$400	1024	10000000000
2^{11}	$800	2048	100000000000
2^{12}	$1000	4096	1000000000000
2^{13}	$2000	8192	10000000000000
2^{14}	$4000	16384	100000000000000
2^{15}	$8000	32768	1000000000000000
2^{16}	$10000	65536	10000000000000000

Bibliography

[1] Gunpei Yokoi; Takefumi Makino. Yokoi Genpai Game Hall Returns: The Creativity that birthed the Nintendo Game Boy (published in Japanese), 2010.

[2] Masaharu Takano. How the Famicom Was Born. *Nikkei Electronics*, Dec. 1994.

[3] Jeremy Parish. NES Creator Masayuki Uemura on the Birth of Nintendo's First Console, 2015. https://www.usgamer.net/articles/nes-creator-masayuki-uemura-on-the-birth-of-nintendos-first-console.

[4] Justin. Atari's Lost Deal for the Nintendo NES, 2004. http://www.atari.io/atari-nintendo-nes-deal/.

[5] Kirby's Development Secrets. http://www.sourcegaming.info/2017/04/19/kirbys-development-secrets/.

[6] Ben Firshman. JSNES - A JavaScript NES Emulator, 2010. https://github.com/bfirsh/jsnes.

[7] Shiru. neslib and CC65 NES examples. https://shiru.untergrund.net/code.shtml.

[8] Patrick Diskin. Nintendo Entertainment System Documentation, 2004. http://www.nesdev.com/NESDoc.pdf.

[9] Nesdev Wiki. http://wiki.nesdev.com/.

[10] Shiru. Programming NES games in C. http://shiru.untergrund.net/articles/.

[11] Dustmop. NES Graphics. http://www.dustmop.io/blog/2015/04/28/nes-graphics-part-1/.

Bibliography

[12] Brad Smith. Lizard Blog.
https://www.kickstarter.com/projects/1101008925.

[13] nesdoug. How to Program an NES game in C.
https://nesdoug.com/.

[14] Kevin Zurawel. Famicom Party.
https://book.famicom.party/.

Some content is licensed under a Creative Commons license:
https://creativecommons.org/licenses/

Index

.word directive, 196
#pragma directive, 160
8-bit architecture, 17
8bitworkshop IDE, 7, 11, 37, 38, 64, 67, 83, 127, 153, 225, 227, 229, 230

6502
    absolute indexed, 178, 185
    addressing mode, 176, 178
    arithmetic, 181
    branch instructions, 180
    condition flags, 179
    indexed indirect, 186
    indirect addressing, 185
    indirect indexed, 185
    logical operations, 183
    loops, 177
    shift operations, 184
    stack, 182
    stack pointer, 182
    zero page, 178
    zero page indexed, 185

actors, 61, 140
address, 14, 23
address bus, 174
address space, 23, 29
address-of operator, 89
addressing mode
    absolute indexed, 211

amplitude, 214
APU, 23, 95, 101, 129, 151, 165, 173, 192, 213
arguments, 40
array lookup, 185
ASCII, 200
asm keyword, 171
ASM6, 229
assembler, 37, 176
assembly, 4, 37, 176, 214
Asset Editor, 38, 47, 61, 227
attribute table, 32, 43, 118, 122, 137, 202
Audio Processing Unit, 23, 95, 151
auto-increment, 88

background, 14, 31, 77
background palette, 32
bank switching, 150, 159, 190, 230
banks, 150
base 16, 18
BCD, 111, 173, 191
binary, 16, 17
binary-coded decimal, 111, 191
bit, 17
bitfield, 132, 141
bitplanes, 30
books
    Making 8-bit Arcade Games in C, 88
    Making Games for the Atari 2600, 173, 188

Index

boolean
    false, 72
    true, 72
break keyword, 135
breakpoint, 10
bus, 23
byte, 17
byte directive, 191
byte keyword, 45

C, 5, 9
ca65, 37, 109, 188
callback, 166
cartridge connector, 25, 149
case keyword, 144
cathode ray tube, 27
cc65, 5, 9, 35, 36, 54, 85,
    170, 188, 228
channels, 95
char keyword, 45
chips
    6502, 2, 4, 191
    RP2A03, 95
CHR RAM, 150, 153, 169,
    190
CHR ROM, 37, 150, 153,
    163, 190, 200
clobbered, 203
clock cycle, 174
collision flag, 81
color cycling, 222
color emphasis, 92
comment tags, 227
companies
    Atari, 3
    Coleco, 3
    Nintendo, 1
    Ricoh, 2

    Sharp, 1
composite video signal, 27
compression, 127, 158
const, 45, 46, 161
const keyword, 45
controller, 71
count byte, 116
CPU clock, 174
CPU vectors, 159, 195
CRT, 27
current VRAM address, 216

D-pad, 2
DASM, 177, 188, 189, 197,
    229
data bus, 174
debugger, 9
decimal flag, 191
delta, 62
delta modulation, 213
dialect, 177
digital-analog converter,
    214
DMA, 206
DMC, 214
double buffering, 158
duty cycle, 96
dynamic RAM, 206

else keyword, 72
emulator, 9
entropy, 86
enum keyword, 133, 140
envelope, 95
equ directive, 187
equate, 187
extern keyword, 117

FamiTone2, 105, 107, 147, 213, 214, 228
FamiTracker, 107, 109, 228
fceux, 226, 228
fine X scroll, 217
flags, 177
for keyword, 63
format string, 80
four-screen mirroring, 152
frame buffer, 154
frame counter, 95
frequency, 96
function, 51
functions
    apu_init(), 97
    bank_bg(), 59
    bank_spr(), 59
    check_scroll_down(), 141
    check_scroll_up(), 141
    draw_actor(), 143
    draw_floor_line(), 134
    draw_stars(), 171
    draw_text(), 162
    famitone_init(), 109
    famitone_update(), 108, 109
    fill_buffer(), 122
    get_floor_yy(), 141
    getchar(), 89
    getntaddr(), 137
    main(), 14, 39, 40, 45, 52, 53, 55, 62, 67, 79, 147
    make_floors(), 133
    memset(), 80
    monobitmap_split(), 156

move_actor(), 146
move_player(), 146
new_segment(), 121, 126
nmi_set_callback(), 166
nt2attraddr(), 125, 126, 138
oam_clear(), 61
oam_hide_rest(), 64, 69, 170
oam_meta_spr(), 67
oam_meta_spr_clip(), 68
oam_meta_spr_pal(), 67, 68, 144
oam_size(1), 70
oam_spr(), 63, 64, 82, 84, 170
pad_poll(), 72, 75
pad_state(), 75
pad_trigger(), 75
pal_all(), 60, 61
pal_bg(), 45, 60
pal_bright(), 94
pal_col(), 14, 40, 45, 60
play_music(), 103
play_scene(), 147
ppu_off(), 16
ppu_on_all(), 61, 91
ppu_wait, 55
ppu_wait_frame(), 16, 54, 55, 64, 69, 80, 83, 84, 94
ppu_wait_nmi(), 55, 69, 83, 89, 127
put_attr_entries(), 125, 126
put_str(), 52

rand(), 62, 85, 86
rand16(), 85
rand8(), 85, 121, 122
refresh_sprites(), 144, 146
rescue_scene(), 147
rndint(), 86, 133
scroll(), 54, 55
scroll_demo, 80
scroll_demo(), 53
scroll_left(), 126, 127
set_attr_entry(), 122, 123
set_metatile(), 121, 122
set_scroll_pixel_yy(), 139, 141
set_shifted_pattern(), 154
set_vram_update(), 79
setup_graphics(), 63, 67
sfx_init(), 109
split(), 83, 84, 89, 156, 219
splitxy(), 219
sprintf(), 80
strlen(), 51, 52
type_message(), 147
update_offscreen(), 126
vram_adr(), 14, 41, 46, 47, 77, 89, 117, 153
vram_fill(), 46, 47
vram_read(), 89
vram_unlz4(), 118
vram_unrle(), 117
vram_write(), 14, 41, 46, 77, 87, 153
vrambuf_clear(), 79, 127

vrambuf_flush(), 79, 80, 146
vrambuf_put(), 79, 80, 124

game systems
    Advanced Video System, 3
    Famicom, 2
    Game & Watch, 2
    NES, 3
games
    Climber, 131, 132, 134
    Donkey Kong, 2, 3
    Duck Hunt, 4
    Gyromite, 4
    Shiru's Chase Game, 90
    Siege Game, 88, 99, 109
    Solarian, 98, 154, 169
    Super Mario Bros., 4
global variable, 54

hardware multiplication, 151
header file, 62
header files, 36
hex, 18
hexadecimal notation, 18
hexdump, 116
horizontal mirroring, 50, 83
horizontal sync, 28

IDE, 7
if keyword, 54, 72
incbin directive, 200, 222
include directive, 188
include files, 188
    peekpoke.h, 161
increments, 198

Index

iNES header, 83, 149, 153, 160, 189, 200
infinite loop, 15
inline assembly, 156, 166, 171
integer overflow, 20
interlacing, 27
interrupt, 40, 183
interrupt flag, 166
interrupt request, 151, 165, 191, 195
IRQ, 84, 151, 165, 191, 195, 215

jitter, 224
JSNES, 9, 67, 152, 226
JSON, 227

kilobyte, 19

label, 177
length counter, 95, 98
LFSR, 85
linear-feedback shift register, 85
link, 189
link directive, 38
linker, 37, 163
listing file, 37
little-endian, 176
local labels, 197
local variable, 15, 53, 54, 62
luminance, 32
LZ4, 118

machine code, 176
macro, 14, 36, 41, 67, 73, 97, 125, 163, 190, 196, 198

main loop, 129
main(), 15
makechr, 221, 222, 228
mapper, 5, 25, 149, 153, 189
    MMC3, 159, 165
    MMC5, 151
    NROM, 153, 190
    UxROM, 153
memory map, 23
Mesen, 226, 228
metasprite, 64, 65, 143, 207
metatiles, 118, 120, 135
MIDI, 107
mirrored, 151
mirroring, 50, 149, 190, 219
mnemonic, 176
modulo, 20, 80, 86, 137, 139

nametable, 14, 31, 39, 41, 43, 49, 77, 88, 90, 199
Nametable Start Address, 216
Nametables, 116
NES Screen Tool, 116, 228
NESASM, 229
NesDev, 228
NESICIDE, 228
NESLib, 5, 13, 36, 89, 129, 161, 229
nibbles, 18, 111
NMI, 40, 151, 165, 193, 195, 202
NMI handler, 89, 94, 108, 129, 211
non-maskable interrupt, 165, 195

251

NTSC, 27, 55, 213, 225
null terminator, 199

OAM, 33, 57, 129, 224
OAM buffer, 62, 170
OAMDMA, 205
object files, 37
offscreen, 119
opcode, 176
operand, 176
org directive, 189, 190, 196
overflow, 180
overscan, 28

page, 206
PAL, 27, 55, 213
palette, 30, 40, 44
palette fades, 93
parallax scrolling, 158
pattern table, 13, 30, 31, 37, 118, 169, 200
PCM, 214
peeking, 162
people
    Gunpei Yokoi, 1
    Hiroshi Yamauchi, 1
    Katsuyah Nakawaka, 2
    Masahiro Sakurai, 4
    Masayuki Uemura, 2
    Shiru, 36, 116, 229
period, 85
Picture Processing Unit, 15, 23, 27
pipeline, 35
pixel clock, 223
pixels, 27
pointer, 133
poking, 162

power of two, 19, 133
PPU, 15, 23, 27, 39, 165
ppu_mask(), 91
preprocessor, 36
preprocessor define, 61, 83, 153, 160
preprocessor directive, 36
PRG RAM, 23
PRG ROM, 23, 95, 150, 159, 190
processor 6502 directive, 188
pseudorandom number generator, 85

RAM, 29
registers, 29, 174
reload value, 165
relocatable, 37
return keyword, 88
return type, 39, 88
Ricoh 2A03, 173
RLE, 115, 228
ROM, 4
run-length encoding, 115
runtime, 35

scanlines, 27
screen color, 32
screen split, 81, 130, 151, 169
scrolling, 31, 49
seed, 85
seg directive, 190
seg.u directive, 189
segment, 120, 132, 160, 189
serial, 71
shadow register, 40, 45, 55, 91

Index

shift register, 209
signed, 19, 62
signed vs. unsigned, 19
single-screen mirroring, 152
sizeof keyword, 46
sliding-window compression, 118
sprite palette, 32, 60
sprite shuffling, 68
sprite zero, 81, 156, 165, 215, 218, 219, 224
sprites, 33, 57
stack, 182
stack pointer, 191
standard library, 35, 85
stripe, 118
struct, 132
struct keyword, 132
subroutine keyword, 197
sweep, 96
switch keyword, 143
system palette, 32

tag byte, 116
temporary VRAM address, 216
tilemaps, 115
title screen, 90
tracker, 107
truncated, 20, 22
two's complement, 19
typedef keyword, 132

uninitialized segment, 189
unsigned, 19, 45

VBLANK, 28, 146

vertical blank, 28, 40, 55, 77, 88, 89, 118, 128, 129, 165, 192, 194, 215
vertical mirroring, 51, 83
vertical sync, 28
video RAM, 24, 88, 153
virtual bright, 93
VRAM, 24
VRAM buffer, 77, 79, 89, 118, 120, 121, 123, 127, 129, 137

while keyword, 42, 54, 63, 68, 127
Wine, 107
wireframe graphics, 158
wrapping, 180

YY-CHR, 228

zero page, 189

253

Printed in the USA
CPSIA information can be obtained
at www.ICGtesting.com
CBHW071316010724
10944CB00012B/134

9 781075 952722